On The Road with Cassadys

&

Furthur Visions

Praise for The Author

"I just LOVE the way you write. Your wit and turns of phrase and insights are so unique and beyond compare. You must write many books!"

Carolyn Cassady
(wife of Neal and love of Jack's life)

"Brian Hassett tells stories like no other, and this book of adventures with my family does not disappoint. I recommend all of Brian's books for fun, energetic jaunts that will keep you entertained and uplifted. Brian does us Proud!"

Cathy Cassady
(daughter of Neal & Carolyn Cassady)

"My God, you're the very spirit of Jack! He would've *loved* you!"

Edie Kerouac Parker
(Kerouac's first wife)

"This is an exceptionally fine piece of work on your part. Marvelous dissertations and mightily written rapportage!"

Henri Cru
(Remi Boncoeur in *On The Road*)

"I like your distinctive narrative voice. You are a great stylist."

Sterling Lord
(Kerouac & Kesey's literary agent)

"Hombre, let me say right off – you are a hell of a writer! This piece you wrote is just wonderful. I love it! It felt like I was there ..... what a treat."

Walter Salles
(director of *On The Road*)

"You're not an *On The Road* scholar — you're an *On The Road* character!"

Teri McLuhan
(Marshall McLuhan's author/filmmaker daughter)

"You can write your ass off!!"

David Amram
(Kerouac's principal musical collaborator)

More Praise for The Author

"Brian Hassett is definitely NOT a typical scholarly researcher! Instead, like all good gonzo reporters, he set out on a personal journey to immerse himself in the movement that started with the Beats, went through the hippies, and has reached into so many corners of America. His memoirs are fascinating, must-read reporting for anyone -- from students writing term papers to young seekers searching for the meaning of life."

Lee Quarnstrom
(author, journalist & original Merry Prankster)

"I am so impressed by Brian's understanding of what he wrote. Other people have knowledge, but he really 'got it.' His impressions of those I know and love were lessons for me, too. He is an astute, keep-it-simple-&-real author ... and I'm proud to also say a Friend."

Anonymous
(aka Linda Breen, original Merry Prankster, who got On The Bus in Calgary in 1964)

"The stories of your adventures are always intriguing and fun. Despite what's going on in the moment — you have an outlook on the world that is just joyful. And I love your play with words."

Jerry Cimino
(founder & curator of The Beat Museum)

"You make lightning strike."

Brad Kepperley
(Aretha Franklin's horn player)

"If it's happiness you want, Brian Hassett seems to have found it."

Bill Sass
(Edmonton Journal)

"People like you are extremely helpful and inspiring."

Susan Ray
(widow of film director Nicholas Ray)

Merry Pranksters' Praise for

The Hitchhiker's Guide to Jack Kerouac

"I'm reading your book and enjoying it immensely. Surprised and enlightened. I'm still laughing from what I read last night. Laughter is the best medicine, and you gave me some big howls. The repartee is so well rendered, and your Ken Babbs descriptions are right on. And very funny. The general mayhem aspect is also spot on. Thanks for the rerun! I was there for part of it with Barlow. Congratulations on creating an awesome read. And thanks for the blast of light! You rock!"

Mountain Girl (Carolyn Garcia)

"When you meet Brian through his words, you will know right away why we like travelling and doing things with him. It's not just what he does, but how he does it. You'll see. And it's how he describes it. He writes the way he talks, and lives the way he writes. Which reminds me of my Dad and Uncle Jack."

John Cassady
(only son of Neal & Carolyn Cassady)

"If you have read Kerouac, and are interested in his life and work, and the movement he and his friends inspired, and the effect it has had on our lives since, I suggest reading Brian's fine book. If you have not read Kerouac, I suggest you do so."

George Walker
(Hardly Visible)

"All the details were perfectly right on — which is so rare and admirable — and appreciated by people like me who are irritated by mistakes. Almost universally writers get one thing or another 'off' or backwards or off to one side. I'll put a book down if I find one or more — but I read yours non-stop right to the end as soon as I started it. It was quite the book!"

Roy Sebern
(original Merry Prankster who first painted
"Furthur" on the front of The Bus)

"This is good stuff."

Zane Kesey (son of Ken & Faye)

On The Road with Cassadys

& Furthur Visions

Brian Hassett

Gets Things Done Publishing

ISBN: 978-0-9947262-2-3

First Edition – Sept. 2018 – Lowell Celebrates Kerouac
Second Edition — June 2019 — West Coast Tour
Third Edition — July 2020 — The *Blissful* Revolution

Front cover photo — John Allen Cassady & author on the balcony of The Rock n Roll Hall of Fame in Cleveland, Nov. 18th, 2012. Photographer unknown.

"The Grateful Dead: Jack Manifested as Music" first appeared in *Kerouac On Record*, Bloomsbury Academic, 2018. Reprinted by permission.
"Floating Universities: The Power of The Collective" first appeared in *The Rolling Stone Book of The Beats*, Rolling Stone Press, 1999. Reprinted by permission.
"Abstract Expression: From Bird to Brando" first appeared in *The Rolling Stone Book of The Beats*, Rolling Stone Press, 1999. Reprinted by permission.
"The Northport Report" first appeared in *Beat Scene*, #39. Reprinted by permission.
"The *On The Road* Scroll Auction" first appeared in Bob Holman's *About Poetry*, June 2001. Reprinted by permission.
Cover design and production by the Michelangelo of books — David Wills.

The book's large 12-point font and open space is intentional. Books should be fun and easy to read and not a chore. You're welcome.

For more information and to stay up to date go to . . .

BrianHassett.com

Facebook.com/Brian.Hassett.Canada

or email — **karmacoupon@gmail.com**

Dedicated to a kindred spirit
and fellow storytelling raconteur

John Allen Cassady

and all my Road and Show collaborators
over the decades

THE HAIKU OF CONTENTS

Part Three — Neal Cassady & the Evermore

All this Merry Prankster stuff that endures decade after decade, it all began with the Beats, with Jack Kerouac, Neal Cassady, Allen Ginsberg, William Burroughs and all their friends, and all their strange intuitive literary works that are still being read to this day. In the spirit of that, and with Neal Cassady joining with Kesey and me and the rest of the Pranksters, there was a flow of energy that was continuous.

I remember a time, 1982, Kesey & Babbs & I drove Kesey's old beat-up green Pontiac convertible all the way from Pleasant Hill Oregon to Boulder Colorado to take part in a conference held on the 25th anniversary of the publication of Kerouac's famous incredible novel *On The Road*. We were there in some way as having sort of inherited the mantle of this literary and psychic ongoing freeing movement that we were all part of.

While we were there, we met a man, a young man, who, although young in years, was broad in mind, and clear of vision. So clear of vision that he hitchhiked all the way from Vancouver B.C., and then wrote a fantastic book about that experience.

Brian Hassett is that man, and he has made it his life's work to continue to present to all of us the insights of the Beats and the Pranksters, and all the history, all the important things that came out of that, which have been perpetuated by the incredible vision, the incredible energy, of this man who is now one of our prime spokesmen, and we are so fortunate for that.

I didn't see Brian again until 2016, but I had somewhat followed his exploits and realized he had become one of the premier Beat and Kerouac scholars in the world. I knew that he was appearing at events and such, but I didn't know what he was doing until this Prankster gathering in Indiana where I saw him perform, and it flat blew me away. I had *no idea* what he could do. I just thought he was a scholar, he writes, he reads, but he doesn't just write, he doesn't just read, he writes like a maniac, and *creates* when he reads. He brings what he's reading absolutely to *life* in the room, and I was stunned. I hadn't seen people perform like that probably since Kesey.

Afterwards, I said, "Wow! That was incredible." And he thanked me, and we got to talking, and I don't recall exactly how it came up, but I said I could read Neal Cassady, and he said, "Oh really?" The next morning he showed up with some pages he'd blown up and color highlighted of this beautiful Jack and Neal dialog right out of *On The Road,* and he handed it to me and said, "Here — read this." And so I did. He didn't know I could become Neal, and I didn't know that he could become Jack. And that began something we've been doing ever since.

I was so privileged to see him on a stage with words. He taught me so much about how to *do* this craft, what it's like to *not* just get up and read something, but to actually *perform* it and bring it to life. He's been doing this stuff for years and years and is one of the most amazing, most skilled people at it in the entire world, I'm absolutely certain.

George Walker
author, performer and original Merry Prankster

Introduction by

S.A. Griffin

In the beginning was the network, and the net was the word weaving all things within the binary web of its electronic wonder. Still a nascent wild-eyed toddler barely out of its DOS diapers, the Internet of the mid-'90s could generally be experienced as an expanding universe populated primarily by email, dry academia and porn. Long before the digital coming of age of the 21st century exploded and corporations began carving the foreboding darkness of the Internet into space cakes, there was the Beat-L: Beat Generation List established May 20, 1995 by Brooklyn College librarian, visionary and Internet pioneer, Bill Gargan. The Beat-L was an email list dedicated to "the study of the lives and works of the writers of the Beat Generation" that included some of great OG Beat luminaries of the time, and those yet to be — an open forum where members could drink freely from the source, get schooled by some of the greats and create new bonds. Ahead of its time in many ways, it sadly flamed out almost three years later on March 27, 1998, the victim of open acrimonious battling over the fate of Jack Kerouac's estate, only a year after the loss of Beat progenitor and great father Allen Ginsberg. Holy the hallucinations and miracle of the Internet! Holy the eternal poet and kindness of the soul!

The glorious Beat-L is the playground where I first encountered my pal Brian Hassett, an electric Prankster and beatific tuning fork that never stops vibrating his great love for life and an even greater love for the Beat Generation, my Canadian bop brother from another beatnik mother.

And so, as it happens, back before blogs ruled their flat world, the phone rang and I answered. It was Brian, enthusiastically recruiting me to help celebrate his 50th Anniversary coast-to-coast Kerouac roast. And this is how our life on the road began, and I was lucky enough to partner with Brian as co-producer for the western end of his 50th Anniversary Kerouac Tour de Scroll.

Cut to: a couple of nights before the show. I arrived in the wee small hours at the Marina del Rey hotel where they were staying. I was on the ready, packing illegal smiles and a cold six-pack of love, prepared for my first face to face with Brian and fellow road warrior John Allen Cassady — who is no doubt, his father's son, as it seems the jazz apple hadn't landed too far from the bop tree.

We popped the tops and burned the crop. Sparks flew as we streamed late into the night and into the first light of day, exploding across the hours, Brian and John with enough energy between them to light up a small coastal city with the atomic glow of their dimension shifting cranial guitars. And the narrative would only increase when we converged at the Short Stop on Sunset Blvd., pages in hand, where we would find the ghost of old Dean Moriarty doing shots with Jack the Forever K, belly up to the former cop bar, writing poems into the ecstatic eyes of night shouting, "Yes!," to the mad existential fathers we would never know.

Brian's joyous recounting of his *On The Road* Scroll adventure with Cassady & company moves along at an amiable clip down their anniversary road spinning a great tale as he takes the reader on his tour of words, beginning in the pre-9/11 era of MTV in The Big Apple of New York City and rolling west to the City of Angels, with Brian and John crashing the shake, rattle and roll of land's end Los Angeles, cavorting and canoodling the stuff that dreams are made of. A world-class raconteur worthy of the Beat mantle, Brian lays it down very fluid, his river of words washing over you like he is standing in the room telling the story to you himself, bouncing about with a beer in one hand, a joint in the other, and an unflagging song in his heart.

Those who buy and read Brian's work will be very pleased.

For the uninitiated, *"walk right in, sit right down... daddy, let your mind roll on..."*

S.A. Griffin
Los Angeles, CA
June 19, 2018

lyrics from *Walk Right In* by Gus Cannon

Explanatory

I've wanted to write a tribute to two of my best Adventure pals, Carolyn & John Cassady, since before the first tales included here, but back in those days I was working full-time at MTV and living in Distraction Central, NYC, and it wasn't until now that the time and sitch synched in. The pieces in this book were written over a 17 year period (there's that number again!) — April 2001 through July of 2018.

The first four stories took place in the four months of April to July in the eventful year of 2001 — including the 50th anniversary of Jack Kerouac writing *On The Road*; the record-breaking auction of that original scroll; and the 40th anniversary shows for him writing *Big Sur*.

I've added some background to open each piece to let you know when they were written and some other context, and have left all largely untouched because — First Thought, Best Thought — that's how the stories were originally told — including language, tone, details & perspective.

Carolyn was one of the smartest, most well-read — and yet FUN! — people I've ever known; and John was one of the kindest, most compassionate — and yet FUNNY! — people I've ever been lucky enough to call a friend.

I hope through these stories I'm able to bring them a little bit to life for those who didn't know them — and maybe inspire John to continue writing his uniquely Cassadyan stories, and perhaps even return to the stage and his rightful place as a primary living voice of the Beat Generation.

I have had the great privilege of prowling around Manhattan with Brian Hassett, who is amazing and special in many ways. Here's a Brian story — which I don't think I've ever told him before — that helps explain it.

I remember several years ago when he and I and my sister Sharon were going to Madison Square Garden for a reunion concert of Crosby, Stills, Nash & Young (a concert that turned out to be really great). As usual, the guards at the Garden had everybody in a line so they could get checked for bottles, weed, pipes, etc. Now, weed and pipes are easy to hide, but I happen to know that Brian is packing a full bottle of Heineken that he doesn't want to part with. He's in front of me and I'm wondering how he's going to pull this off. He hides it in his coat, and when the lady with the electric wand spots it he smiles and says, "Oh, that's just my beer."

Here's the amazing part: she waves him in.

As a writer, Brian has the same amazing skill. He's disarmingly easygoing and always has a big grin on his face, but he absolutely knows where he's going and why, and whatever emotions or meanings or memories he's trying to smuggle in, you can count on it that he will. That's how Brian Hassett writes.

Marc Eliot Stein
aka Levi Asher, founder of Litkicks.com,
the first Beat website
New York City
July 17, 2018

Part One

John Allen Cassady

and The Jackroad

1

Howlin' at the Jackmoon

Beginning in the mid '90s I started producing a series
of shows in various clubs in lower Manhattan that
featured all sorts of famous and unfamous writers and
performers. Back then, I always intended to write a
story about one of the shows — capture at least one in a
written form to have a record of what we did. Of all of
those 20 or 30 shows, this On The Road celebration was
the most fun, the most hassle-free, the highest & purest
energy. It was my happy surprise when I discovered
nearly 20 years later that I'd actually written the story
of that night — found on a floppy disk and recovered
from an old version of Word. This is mostly unchanged
from the obvious post-show enthusiasm with which it
was written.

Event: 50th Anniversary of Jack starting writing the On
    The Road *scroll*
Date: Monday, April 2nd, 2001
Location: Chelsea Commons, 24th Street & 10th Avenue,
    Manhattan
Written: April – May, 2001

I first re-met Jack not long after my girlfriend and I split up. I had just gotten over a serious depression that I won't bother to talk about, except that it had something to do with the miserably weary break-up and my feeling that everything was dead. With the second coming of Jack Kerouac began the part of my life you could call my life on the road.

It was the dawn of the millennium and I was working full-time at MTV in Times Square as an Executive Aide-de-Camp, so I was completely immersed in the entertainment world. My desk had a subscription to every imaginable entertainment magazine, and we got an inch-thick stack of daily press clippings every morning from every place one of our networks appeared in print. It was a full-time job — or distraction — to read those things every day. Plus there were TVs tuned to the entertainment channels all over the building, and every person you talked to was not only surfing the showbiz wave, but often helping shape it.

One day in this milieu at this time in history, I read a story about something that was going to have its 50th anniversary in the year 2000. That's when it first twigged.

"Oh my God, it's soon gonna be the 50th anniversary of . . . *everything that ever happened!*" Raising my eyes off the page and staring into the empty space out the 28th floor midtown windows, I started to think about the 50th anniversary of ... *The Wild One ... Rock Around The Clock ... Rebel Without A Cause ... **On The Road!!***

"*I gotta ride this!* This is gonna be so fun!" And the question immediately hit — what was *the first* important cultural event of the 1950s?

Of course! Jack Kerouac sitting down to write *On The Road* on a single scroll of paper in 20 days — starting April 2nd, 1951.

That's all I needed to hear!

A 2000s view of 454 West 20th Street
in Chelsea, Manhattan, New York.

After work that day, the first thing I did was go to the house where he wrote it. 454 West 20th Street — a nice 4-story red-brick walk-up in Chelsea. I thought, "I'm gonna wanna be here that night. (pause) And I bet Walter (Raubicheck) and Levi (Asher) would want to too. (pause) We should make a night of it." And that's pretty much how The Trip began.

I thought about getting a permit for a street party on the block ... but knew that would be more red tape than fun. If there'd been a park in front of the building, maybe we coulda done a nice event there. But there wasn't. So I walked to the nearest corner, 10th Avenue, but was Froze Out looking for the perfect neighborhood bar or venue on the corner.

Where would Jack go? WWJD? Look at this corner, look at that corner, as I inched my way uptown carefully along the avenue he would have walked so many times — looking for the closest space to throw a party in the old boy's honor on the anniversary of the day he began changing history forever.

Finally — it took all the way up to 24th & 10th to find the first possible joint — the Chelsea Commons — a neighborhood bar & restaurant — with a ceilingful of psychedelic florescent puppets that I knew would begin to dance as the night got weird. Went in, talked to the owner. "No, we don't do 'shows' here."

Ha! He hadn't met *me* yet!

We went down to his New York bar basement "office" full of cases of beer and boxes of food and a thousand years of papers scattered like a hurricane . . .

4

and I explained how that front corner by the windows was really a stage . . . and how some lights could be pointed just a little different . . . and how we're talkin about a Monday night in April . . . and I'd have the place packed to the rafters for 5 or 7 hours . . . and bring in an all-star line-up . . . and how it's for neighborhood hero Jack Kerouac, who, God bless, the owner knew of and thought highly of — and Boom! the show was on!

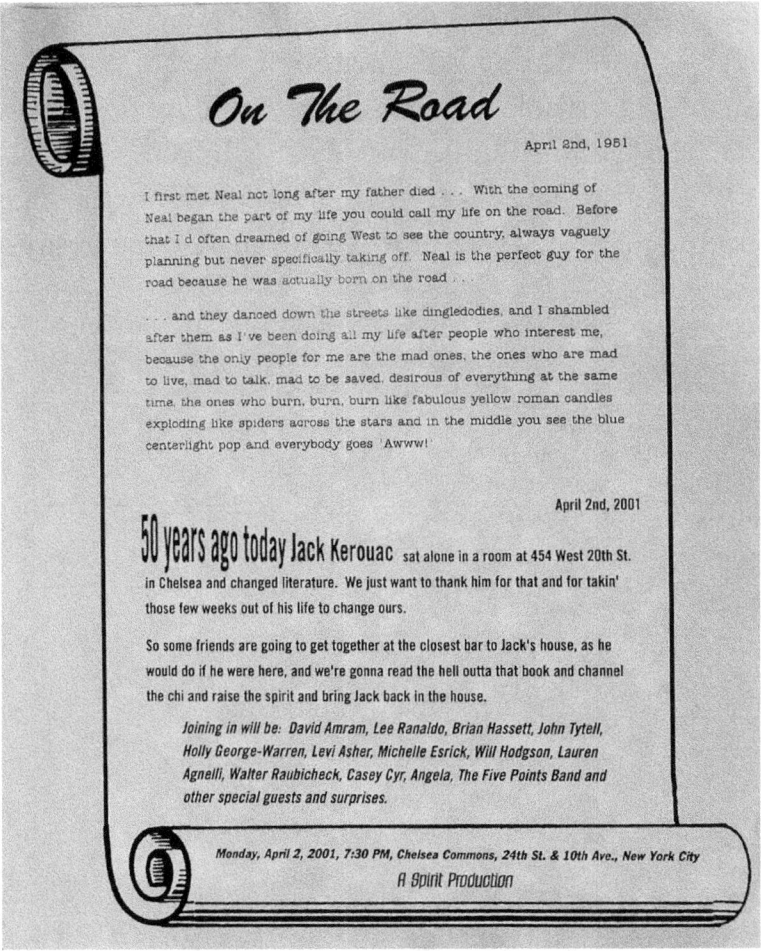

The scroll poster for The Scroll show.

I ended up looping in Jack's principal musical
collaborator David Amram; Sonic Youth's Lee Ranaldo;
Kerouac biographer and all-round Beat scholar John
Tytell; film director Michelle Esrick in the middle of
making her documentary *Saint Misbehavin'* about
Wavy Gravy; my original Winnipeg music partner Will
Hodgson; Literary Kicks (LitKicks) founder Levi Asher
(aka Marc Stein); playwright and professor Walter
Raubicheck; raconteur musician Robin "The Hammer"
Ludwig and his Five Points Band; Greenwich Village
singer-songwriter and Washington Square Lauren
Agnelli, and a whole host of others, including Ken Kesey
and a bunch of his Pranksters! Or . . . almost.

Kesey had a college gig in nearby Albany the night
before . . . or so he thought when he emailed me to say he
was coming.

```
Subj:  Re: Happy 50th, Jack
Date:  3/22/01 2:58:22 PM EST
From:  kenk@efn.org (kesey and/or babbs)
Reply-to: kenk@efn.org
To:    Karmacoupe@aol.com

          B--
          Some of us will try to make it.
          I have a college gig in Albany on
          (I think) April 1st. Or maybe I
          don't have a gig. Maybe it's just
          some kinda torturous April Fool's
          trick. Who knows...?
          --Kesey

   --

       _/‾‾‾‾‾‾|  http://www.intrepidtrips.com
      |_ FURTHER _|  Box 764 Pleasant Hill OR 97455
        O    O
```

But it turned out he had the dates confused and he was someplace else. *So* too bad. It would have been the perfect bookend of our life with Jack together — which began in the summer of '82 when we both travelled a thousand miles for a good conversation (as Gary Snyder used to say) in Boulder for the Kerouac Super-Summit. As John Clellon Holmes put it: "We had come from all over the country, from all periods of Kerouac's life, and more of us were together than had ever been in one place at one time before." — you can read all about it in *The Hitchhiker's Guide to Jack Kerouac* — and now here we were about to come together again . . . and but for the schedule conflicts we almost did . . . then six months later Ken unexpectedly and inexplicably died. (!) :-(

This Chelsea show ended up being the best of the couple dozen Beat-related shows I produced in New York during those years. With the hard-learned problematic local egos all being dropped from the lineup before the puck-drop, it was an unhampered unhinged joyous ride of a night.

Getting to the gig, I was hitchhiking for so long on the frantic American Lexington Avenue that it felt like I was stumbling in a starvation daze on the streets of San Francisco. With no one stopping to pick me up I got so lonely, so sad, so tired, so quivering, so broken, so beat, that I got up my courage. Slowly I raised my thumb-extended hand from where it was pointing lazily toward the horizon, and began to hold it higher. And as I reached skyward t'ord the heavens, stretching for the Spirit Waves surging just above us, I opened my hand in utter supplication, fingers splayed that I may catch The Force, and Lo! — a big yellow taxi suddenly appeared! "Yeah, this'll work," I thought. "Fuck hitchhiking."

I jumped in and shoved my tattered old rucksack and digi-video camera across the blue vinyl seat. Whadda ya need secret scribbled notebooks for yr own joy for when you can catch it all on a 2-camera digi shoot?

So, we're headin' downtown and I'm drinkin' a beer loaded for deer, headin' for The Chelsea. Commons, that is. Swimming cool, rock stars.

I leapt out of the flying boxcar checker at 20th & 9th. My gut feeling about the show was it would be a glistening many-faceted diamond. This one was gonna be special. But in The Empirical Data Dept. there were fewer emails and phone calls than a regular show, so there was also this weird Empirical Tick in my Head.

I'd scribbled Jack's scroll-writing address all over the place and suggested people gather there before the show. So everybody knew about the house and I was worried more people might hang there than come to our Commons show. I was imagining a sort of John Lennon or Jerry Garcia memorial with candles and handmade cards taped to the fence and girls in peasant dresses sitting cross-legged on the sidewalk next to a guy with a guitar and some kind of sweet leaf smoke wafting between them. I was in quite an *All You Need Is Love* mood as I wheeled around the corner and onto the sidewalk, and it's gotta be right about . . . hmmm. There was one lady walking a dog. And I don't think his name's Cassady if you catch my blank postcard.

Whoa. Nobody loves me. Nobody loves Jack. Woe is the world, and then you die. Mommy. I wanna go home. Though, maybe I better stop at the bar first.

So I was in quite a *Desolation Angels* mood as I wheeled around the corner heading for the Commons where . . . there was an enormous mob of people out front on the sidewalk!

As I walked up — you could see through the big open corner windows that the joint was packed. I had to actually duck down and push myself in through the opening between a woman's waist and the wall, swimming through the mingling sea and plopping onto "the stage." It was live, and it was loud. People everywhere. All the seats were full. P.A. was up, it was 6:45, showtime's 7:30, we're all set! Yeah! . . . Except not one of the musicians were present. The pivotal keyboard was nowhere to be seen. Nothin's been soundchecked. Bebop's *not* playing on the house system. The lights aren't set. And I don't have a drink!

For the next hour there was a lot of hugging, vibing, and some amazing space-crunching New York stage magic on the tiny 6-by-6-foot stage, followed by a funny Three Stooges scene with the owner carting in this old wooden stepladder and setting it up in the middle of the crowded room with all these people crammed onto every tiny jazzbar seat, and him climbing up above them all to re-set the little track spotlights, and I was so freaked that he was actually up there doing it above all this slithering chaos around him that I flashed back to a time I had to do the same thing *after* one of those psychedelic

1970s Acid Tests we did, climbing up to take down microphones we'd hung from the ceiling in the sober pre-show . . . then post-show looking down from the starry ceiling at the pandemonium swirling below like waves on the Sea . . . shoo — shaw — shirsh — roll, roll, swirling the sand twirling floor — back — forth — swish — boom, sway, doom, day — as I was drifting away so contentedly until suddenly this spotlight hit me in the eyes. "Alright, how about that?"

"Oh, yeah, okay, sure." I wanted it over before Curly entered stage left carrying a long plank.

It was about 7:30 at this point. Seemed like most everything was done, except Dave Amram wasn't here yet. I went out to the private back courtyard for a groove-down focus before starting the show. I was the host / emcee / producer / glue. The night, to a large extent, was going to ride on me and how I presented myself and what colors I chose to paint the canvas with. I was the conductor for a spirited disarray of musicians and readers playing in tonight's orchestra. Everything about the tone of the symphony is set by the conductor, and I really wanted an up-tempo happy Beat. At my most recent gig the week before I'd just bombed. Worst show of my life it felt like. No connection with the audience. Probably my fault. So I knew I better have the right channel tuned in tonight.

Out there in the courtyard I was frozen with ecstasy on the cobblestones. I didn't know whether I was here or back in a courtyard in 1750 in England! I was in New York now, only in another life, and in another body.

"Noooo," the muse seemed to say with her terrific beam. "You have come back for Jack. He's here. And he's happy. Very happy . . . that you held this anniversary at a bar. He's in there right now with a shot and a beer."

So I bolted back inside and started the show. "Let's get this goin' early so at least some of us will remember at least part of it," I said into the microphone as I called for the bartender to turn down the jukebox. And just as I was getting the attention of the disparate desperados in the familio, in through the stage-side doors burst **David Amram!** Boom! Bang! Pop! And everybody goes 'Awwww'! French horn case bouncing off flute case bouncing off bar railing bouncing off self, bursting into the crowded club and onto the tiny stage with electric Jack energy sizzling off him. The train had just begun to chug out of the station and here was Sunny Dave throwing his instruments in the open boxcar door and pullin' himself aboard. The Kero-crew was complete. Commence combustion.

And as we lifted off, I set the scene of Jack's hard work in historical spring 1951 perspective: the Korean War was raging, the Rosenbergs had just been convicted and sentenced to death this very week, and it was President Truman in office, not Eisenhower as is so often associated with Jack & the Beatstocks. Also — 2001 was synchronistically the same calendar year as 1951, so Jack actually started his new writing job on a Monday, just as it fell this year.

And just for fun during these 20 days in any April — you can figure out roughly what he was writing each day, averaging around 15 printed pages every day. I'm writing this tale six days after he started it, so he was probably writing the whole Mill City section with Henri Cru (Remi Boncoeur) this weekend, which to me is some of the funniest stuff in the book. (Pssst, glad you had a happy weekend, Jack!)

Anyway, back to the essentials, which, also by way of set-up before we got to the *Road* fiction, I read Jack's *Essentials of Spontaneous Prose*, which he wrote as a direct result of writing *On The Road* and *The Subterraneans* so quickly that Allen asked him to write down how he got it down.

And in the Spirit of full show disclosure, I also tossed in Jerry Garcia's classic quote from the Rhino box set book about — "I can't separate who I am now from what I got from Kerouac. I don't know if I would ever have had the courage or the vision to do something outside with my life — or even suspected the possibilities existed — if it weren't for Kerouac opening those doors."

Dave Amram said he also wanted to do a little Opening Blessing, so I turned the altar over to The Senior Spirit, and Pops began to blow his magic dust all over the room, reading the "Love your lives out" part from Jack's *Origins of the Beat Generation*, and rapping about sharing, then blowing out the gentle Lakota *Round Dance Ladies' Choice* to summon the spirits into the house.

Once the choir and the angels were harmonizing, we began with the opening lines Jack typed this very day 50 years ago: "I first met Neal not long after my father died . . ." with each reader doing a quick several-sentence riff, one curvation of *the road* then another driver, all with Amram ridin' shotgun on the keys across his lap playing the soundtrack to our lives of talk since we were old enough to hear, keepin' the acts and scenes in four-four time until the blues band flashed on another rhyme, and assorted drummers fell in, wailin' on a multi-voiced choir singing the fabulous exploding yellow roman candle opening chapter until **Lee Ranaldo** and I finished it off in holy blessed sweetness with the "Somewhere along the line I knew there'd be girls, visions, ev-ery-thing; somewhere along the line the pearl would be handed to me."

Then the great teacher preacher **John Tytell** read that scat discovery-of-jazz passage where Dean and Sal go out on the town in ol' S.F., Dean fully diggin' every moment and Jack laying down every nuance with every jazz-juicy sentence. (Which you can also hear the author himself read on the 1999 Jim Sampas/Lee Ranaldo-produced *Jack Kerouac Reads On The Road* CD.) So there's John howling at the Jackmoon with Amram jammin, pullin' out the French horn, holdin' it high like the Five Spot photos, and takin' us all higher, takin' it furthur than he'd gone before, building John's howling reading into a long sweet jazzy jam.

From Tytell's animated grey-bearded jazz horn yelping, I brought up **Angela**, an effervescent Canadian former stripper who knew how to work a room and make people of all persuasions smile. She's also a poet who wrote one of my favorite lines of the year — "I used to be an outlaw until I got in-laws."

She read that part where the boys went into New York for New Year's Eve, the same chapter that leads to the epiphanistic "Hearing Shearing" passage we're gonna peak with later. And I kept thinking about all the different voices and rainbows of colors that spin out of that book as the cute young blond followed the grizzly howling wolf while standing next to curly-haired keyboardist Amram and the be-bowlered bluesman **Robin The Hammer** on guitar.

And then the pollinated bud of rock 'n' roll & the Beats blossomed again as **Sonic Youth's Lee Ranaldo** came up. And in the further continuing synchronicity of the Jacknight, Lee was doing the part where Dean & Sal get to Chicago and go catch some jazz, and he was going to end right at the paragraph that I was going to read climaxing with "Here were the children of the American bop night." Tag-team!

And in the Another Amazing Thing Dept. — I asked a couple people in advance what they were going to perform, but had no idea what most had chosen — just kinda left it in the hands of the Gods — and Lo no two people walked in intending to read the same thing! Jest a grand in-synch groove.

Lee (like Levi Asher) has this kinda low-key natural persona on stage, which is so weird cuz they both wear tons of make-up and sparkly disco clothes off stage. Okay, that last part may be an improvised extrapolation of inexactitude, but the point is, in honest Neil Young fashion, Lee took us strolling on this roaming jazz journey through downtown Chicago with Downtown Dave rippin' jazz licks on the piano on one side and bobbin' Robin riffin' Chicago Blues on the other as the Chicago music tales were playing out all around him. I crouched down beside the stage on the bar rail where you normally put your foot (and where the word "bar" came from to mean drinking establishment) and there I sat like a base drum secretly keeping the Beat and taking it all in.

And that was the thing about the night — not simply were we reading Jack, but everybody in the room had so internalized the friendly open spirit of the book & scene that everyone knew what to do instantly and instinctively — an overt friendliness transcending everything.

I followed Lee's section, where Jack steps out of the story to tell the history of bop, and there's supposed to be this seamless transition, but Lee was so fuckin' rockin' everyone clapped and the band stopped playing which is what you get for improvising the set-list on the spot. But Lee had taken it up a notch or three and the room was vibrating and I could feel from the stage it was really "up" so I just let 'er rip — this being one of the passages that Jack used to read with juice and David performs regularly whenever he does a Kerouac segment at one of his shows.

One afternoon, back when I didn't have a job and could do cool stuff in the midweek afternoons, Dave was doing this big Figaro Cafe anniversary show down at Bleecker & MacDougal — the crossroads of Greenwich Village. There was all this media there, and everybody was in a great groove — in fact it was the day Levi Asher and I first bonded on those empty ghost-town Village afternoon streets. As Dave began his show, he started introducing this guy from Canada who's written a book, and I was like, "Oh there's another Canadian writer here?!" as I craned my neck to see if I recognized anyone. Then he mentioned "*The Temp Survival Guide*" and I was like, "Oh. There probably aren't two of those."

I had about what? maybe 2 seconds to get ready to go on. Hmmm. And B) what are we gonna perform? So I grabbed the piece I was working on that day and I ran up in front of all the rolling cameras and rocking circus, and Dave says, "Where's the piece Adira gave you?"

I says, "What piece?"

"Oh. . . . . . . Adira! Where are those copies of the
Jack scripts?" And this little glitchoid went for forever-
and-a-half with me just standing there in the spotlight,
and it was funny cuz I'd been circulating with everyone
in the room beforehand and then Boom all of a sudden
I'm as surprised as anyone that I'm standing at the
microphone. It took forever to find the pages but finally
she hands me *A Long Day's Journey Into Night*, and
I was like, "This is a Long play." So she hands me the
aforementioned "Children of the American Bop Night"
paragraph. So you see, there was a point to all this.

Then Boom! with local news crews rollin' I
performed this long paragraph I hadn't looked at in ages
and it was one of those — you've got nothing to lose — an
impossible position — something's handed to you with
no preparation — and, *"You'rrre on . . . !"* "Okay, here
we go," and I just went for it, sending it out broadcast
to rock the jazz world. Somehow an internal rhythm
came into my head, maybe it was David's music, but we
found the groove and took it on a wild dynamic ride —
until we eeeeased 'er down into the sweet-climax ending
with a prayerful whisper: "Here were the children of the
American bop night."

So there I was facing the throbbing Chelsea
Jacknight crowd after Lee'd wowed 'em and the race
car was purring and I just took that bopper for a cruise!
There's lotsa places you can go with this paragraph — go
ahead, try it at home. Beginning, "Once there was Louis
Armstrong ..." [near the start of part 3, ch. 10] and jest let

17

'er rip in your bedroom with your hairbrush microphone and no one home in the middle of a midweek afternoon and let the dynamics swing. You can hear Jack's reading of part of it about 20 minutes into that 28-minute solo reading on that Rykodisc *On The Road* recording. But define it yourself. It's a fun jazzy hit-single Jackgraph you can dance to. And dance we did.

Which was followed by the actress and filmmaker **Michelle Esrick** weaving her magic spell. I knew the room was in professional hands, so after the Louis Armstrong - Lee Ranaldo - Dave Amram combo climax, I slipped out to the secret backyard dressing-room courtyard that even local people told me later they never knew was there. I don't know who was hanging at this point — the night had taken on a trace-like quality — but all night there was a revolving group out there: Angela the stripper, Anthony & Anne from the Cannabis Cup, Andy from MTV who was also in Amsterdam when we inducted Jack & Neal, and an ever-evolving coterie of escapees spilling out from the circus.

In fact, the outdoor courtyard was the skeleton key to unlocking the ghostnight. Surrounded by seven-foot-high brick walls with old Paris and London street signs like "Edith Grove" (which I thought would make a terrific character's name) all with perpetually waving trees overhead under the high street lights that were continually casting swirling shadows over the subterranean cats in their nocturnal lair. I remember looking up into the sky a lot that night. And smiling. You look up when yer Grateful, and it was sure obvious who was up there beaming back.

This was a family reunion for all the Beats in New York, some old faces I hadn't seen in 10 or 15 years, plus a couple'a cats I'd had back-alley hissing fights with who showed up on this soul-special night, and with just a glance, all was forgiven. And this was being repeated in an ongoing hundred-character drama all over the room.

Returning to the show, I had a feeling the current musical line-up was running its course, and there was another monster ensemble scattered around the room, so I decided to orchestrate some musical chairs, which has to take place, mind you, on a stage the size of a table for four. And while I set this in motion, not wanting there to be a lull, for some misguided reason, I stepped up and begin to read the great mid-book San Francisco sidewalk epiphany scene that I first did as part of the marathon *On The Road* reading at St. Mark's Church a couple years back. I thought I'd just fill the empty non-music space with a little reading, but a sentence or two in, could feel everyone needed a break, so I made a fateful call in the fluid flow of battle and called out instead for the bartender to pop on one of the bebop CDs I brought — and *voila!* Instant Intermission! Plus simultaneously saving the epiphany passage for later! The chance for people to re-shuffle and talk is an opening often missing at these sometimes 6 or 8-hour marathon events. You need time for all those — "Phew, what was *that!?*" "Hey, how'd you come to be here?" etceteras.

I remember somebody saying during the break — "You're the most Uptown *and* Downtown person in the scene." I asked, and what she meant was — I was producing / performing at downtown Village clubs every week or month — while also fully entrenched in the successful Uptown skyscraper corporate entertainment business world. In the words of John Cassady, "I'll take it."

Levi Asher hit the mic after the dust settled, and asked Will Hodgson to play with him. You probably know Levi from his Literary Kicks website (litkicks.com), but Hodgson and I have known each other since we were teenagers on the same elm-awninged street in Winnipeg, Manitoba. He and I co-wrote *Smokin' Charlie's Saxophone* about the ghosts of Jack, Neal and Charlie Parker haunting the ancient streets of ol' New York. I could tell you a million stories about ol' Will, but most of them you couldn't print. We've played together for years and he was gung-ho for the show from the get-go just so ya know. Drove all the way from Philly. Or should I say Scott did. Will's a writer who doesn't drive, if you can imagine such a thing. I know in Hodgson's case it's like driving with Picasso where he sees the road as a Cubist abstraction and you never know which facet he might veer off on. Which also describes his playing.

We also brought up **Scott Cunningham** on djembe and **Deborah Reul** on the small kit, and Levi spun his twisted vision across the room. He opened with this whole rap about courage, and honesty, and generosity. Levi has a way of tapping into the deepest current. Where I'm fluttering along on the happy melody line, Levi's always digging down in the deeper bass trenches, and we're always playing off of (or fighting over) these two visions. He's a fuckin' mastermind with more than a few quirky quirks — like he likes to not know exactly where he's going when he goes somewhere so he has to meander around and find things. We have a sibling-like relationship in how we banter and fight back & forth, but since we come from the same core family we're never too far from home — like this cab ride a couple nights earlier going down to Lauren Agnelli's party in the Village. Sister Sharon's sitting in the middle and Levi and I were at the windows having some major debate over the plans for the night and what we should do at each point and we started squawnkin' back & forth in this rapid-fire bebop-paced argument that had Sharon in stitches and the cabbie thinking a fight was about to break out, while Levi and I were both holding in the laughter while we sustained the goof on each other's ferociousness of opinion while still working our way through the melody to the resolution of the evening's song. Kinda like that.

So I introduced him never knowing what old Meanderman was gonna do, and sure enough he pulled out this paragraph that in my old first copy of *On The Road* is marked at the top of the page with the words "Pivotal Point" and half of the paragraph he picked is underlined. Then as he's introducing it he says, "This is kind of a pivotal point in the book." (!) That's what I mean. And he reads something Jack could have written on this very day cuz it's only on about page 15. "I didn't know who I was for about fifteen strange seconds. I wasn't scared; I was just somebody else, some stranger

. . . I was halfway across America, at the dividing line between the East of my youth and the West of my future."

And besides everything that was happening on stage, there was David Amram meeting **Big Tim** for the first time, the hip executor of Henri Cru and Edie Kerouac's estates. And there's Chris from *High Times* talking to transplanted San Francisco Beat comic actor **Mark Lewis**. And there's vivacious Anne from Amsterdam huggin' and kissin' and laughin'. Floats like a butterfly, swings with the Bs. And there's Brian diggin' on all the people and humming on Levi's launch when suddenly he's finished! Ouu, I was enjoying that. Oh yeah. "Outer space to spotlight, come in." Whoops — I'm up. Spring into action. Who's on next? What's on second. I Dunno's on third.

Quick-like-a-buddy — Wally, **Walter Raubicheck**, who wrote the Gregory Corso piece in *The Rolling Stone Book of The Beats*, and I introduced him in part as "my best friend for 20 years," he has the keys to my apt., that sorta thing, but I had no idea. He gets up there, and the giant engine has completed the slow motion chug into propulsion of the mighty train, the locomotive's already movin' and groovin', and into the pocket the Wally rocket fires up, and he cues the band that music is key to reaching the IT, and proceeds to knock out that whole gem-filled passage where Dean and Sal are riding together in the back seat while someone else drives and they have their discussion about Time and IT that Walter delivers in this meteoric explosion that nobody was expecting or thought he had in him — funny, twisted, passionate, and the band just *cranked* it up, heavy on the IT, heavy on the percussive Beat, a driving blues beat, full-groove, the whole room shaking to the multiple drums and the Yes Yes Yes of Dean's excited rap. When Walter peaks with the climactic, "... as Dean and I both swayed to the rhythm and the IT of our final excited joy in talking and living to the blank tranced end of innumerable riotous angelic particulars that had been lurking in our souls all our lives!" the band was just cookin' on their own angelic particulars — and the room was lifting off the ground, soaring close to the zenith.

I knew we could break Mach 1 here, so I pulled out "Hearing Shearing" from the stack of sheets on the music stand, that ecstatic jazz night that left Dean pop-eyed with awe — and without any *hesitation blues* and the drummers still beating, I leapt right into "Dean and I went to see Shearing at Birdland in the midst of the long mad weekend ..." and the whole band just fuckin' *took it* to the next level. I introduced the players using Jack's intro of Shearing's . . . another short snappy two minute single from Jack's opera — one of the passages he used to read with David — so it's familiar and it rocks — and the band's got a groove and the drums were takin' over and the rhythm fell into place as "Shearing comes out, blind, led by the hand to his keyboard" and the place began to whoop! "There he is! That's him! Oh God! Oh God, Shearing! Yes! Yes! Yes!" Dean yelled, as Amram fell into the jam on his talking drum smiling-up a stage and keepin' up the accelerato demento pace we got this race clippin' at. And Professor Brackett stepped up with

another giant djembe right in front of me with this big
round drum just thumpin' at my heart center as we got
into some tribal transcendent groove with Hodgson
laying down some Amadeus Garcia melody lines on
the guitar and me nodding to him as he's following the
rising intensity knowing if we push this puppy faster
harder furthur it'll take us there, all we gotta do is GO as I
pushed my long hair back and I began to sweat. And the
guitar player hunched over and socked it in, faster and
faster, it seemed, faster and faster that's all! And Amram
began to play the skins, and they rolled out of the drum
in great rich showers, you'd think the man wouldn't have
time to line them up. They rolled and rolled like the sea.
Folks yelled for us to "Go!" And Jack was conscious of
the madmen singing him, he could hear every one of our
gasps and imprecations! "That's right!" he screamed,
"YEESSSSSSSSS!"

And there we were in Jackland. Easy as that.

And the band kept grooving, no let down, no
breakdown. There were five or six drummers and the
engine hummin' and the room's screaming and the
drummers still beating and Lauren Agnelli's up next
— though now missing in action . . . the drummers are
calling and the emcee's stalling and the engine's hauling
and there's nobody at the controls and I'm still shaking
from Shearing and bopping from the djembe and swirlin'
on Heineken and dancing on water and can't stop now
— this is what we do it for and I'm callin' for Lauren in a
Beat tribal chant but there is no Lauren, no motion in the
ocean, "Gotta Go!" Dean yelled from somewhere above

me, "Go man Go!" I heard everywhere in the room and reached for that San Francisco epiphany trip we almost took earlier, "Oh yeah, that takes you to the outer limits," and Hodgson's got this wicked groove goin' and I got this okay-I'm-with-ya goin', and point the car San Francisco way cuz somewhere along the line I knew the pearl would be handed to me, all reaffirmed as David re-emerged on the keyboard and started doin' this driving Johnny Johnson '50s honkin' go-for-it piano and we took that 8-minute ride, the hallucination of Jack's mother from 1750s England scolding him until "just for a moment I had reached that point of ecstasy that I always wanted to reach …" as shakers were passed out and the room was filling with rhythm. Musicians flowed around the stage, a massive multi-drumming unstoppable chant like a speeding locomotive's chugging as Jack's solo hugged the ground and took us to "where all the angels dove off and flew into the holy void of uncreated emptiness, the potent and inconceivable radiances shining in bright Mind Essence, innumerable lotuslands falling open in the magic mothswarm of heaven." And there we were — gone. No present. Shakers shakin' the room, puppets' legs shaking the ceiling — Jack's words shakin' us all — and it all flew so nicely into its grounding conclusion, as Jack came back to Marylou's hotel room and had a smoke and admitted, holy shit, "I was way too young to know what had happened."

And so were the rest of us. About the last thing I remember saying into the mic was, "Well, I have _no_ idea where we go from here," to loud laughs at the truth.

And thank the gods there was someone yet to come —
Lauren Agnelli, the musician, poet and Greenwich
Village spirit lo these many years, and she stepped up
to the plate, but at this point I was so spent, so Beat, so
bongo-blasted I retreated to the cool in-more-ways-than-
one courtyard — the solace respite getaway plan — where
ya can't see the trees for the forest of faces beaming in
the enchanted Jacknight like a cluster of night-elves —
cool breeze coolin' down the steamy spotlight glisten
— heart-beating double-vision, kaleidoscope spinning
rotation of friends' faces, of British brick walls and a trip
through time, trippin' on rhyme with bombers and wine,
bringing Jack on back with a conga and trap, opening the
safe with a collective thumb snap, bringing it home with
those who care, waking up the sleeping bear and roaring
aloud in the Chelsea night. Shaking and dreaming in
the immensity of it. No more wishes. Everyone was just
here, Jack included, and there was nothing else left to do
but smile smile smile, and tell more stories and wonder
if it's ever been this good before, and everyone beaming
with the IT. Getting there, got it there, there, IT — ahhh,
in the immensity of it, ah-ha-ing in the intensity of it,
and there's Professor Carl like some Puck elf we never
see but who's lit up like a three-year-old in the fury
of play, saying, "Jack is channeling his spirit through
you." And big Walter beaming down from his basketball
heights having sealed the deal with his slam-dunk game-
breaker and all the other wizards of old and new passing
around sparklers and lighting the crew. A wedding, an
anniversary, a birth day view. I poured the night in my

old pipe and lit up. Man, I was way to young to know what was happening.

At some point Hodgson joined Robin Ludwig and the Five Points Blues Band for that Canned Heat *On The Road Again* Woodstock blues funk, and then the band took 'er for a ride as music drove us into the night, here we go, blow man blow, sailing into the light, with the sculpted porcelain arms of the draft beer taps tipping back and gushing all over the room, and grey-haired arms in tattooed throngs tipping them back in the rapids of the river as the night whooshed by. A collective of collectables gathered in circles in chairs and passed 'round the torch of ecstasy and playing with the light in a dream it would seem.

At one point, they lit into a little *Willie and The Hand Jive*, then the Jack & Neal ghost-ride *Smokin' Charlie's Saxophone* that I wrote years ago and seeing as we were in "a secret pranksters' hideaway" in New York City thinking of Neal and Jack, and ending with Brackett's *Freedom Train*.

And later still, after everything had been shut down twice, Amram comes over to me and says he wants to do another song. By this point I know only the one manager is here who's been kinda bustin' our chops from the git, but I know Dave, and he ain't a bandleader for nuthin'. I've rarely seen him not get his way, and I know this grouchy guy's got it in for us, and there's no way I'm askin' him, but I also know, I smile, if ol' Sunny Dave goes over there Groucho's gonna give. Lasts about 10 seconds. And Dave starts settin' up while still regaling him with tales of gregarious genius.

And so the master maestro commands the stage yet again in the late night ah-ha, and lures the life back outta the night and takes us on a ten-minute *This Song's For You, Jack* with versefuls of improvised lines on the night we're having, on our life, on Jack's light, with Scott Cunningham and Deborah Reul rollicked along on the congas, and the glasses tapped and the room was wrapped in Jack's spirit by his maestro-in-arms in head-boppin' multi-jazz funk. Whoooaaa, brutha-Dave!

Next thing I know I'm over at the bent-elbow corner of the bar ordering pick-me-up margaritas with MTV brother Scott Cunningham as we watch over the scene from our kingly stools shakin' our heads in a "Whoa, what was that?!?" fun-stunnery. Like two writers sitting back and looking over what they'd written, after

The Two in The City.

all these years of Scott and I talking of working together, we're finally glowing in technicolor spades, as we watch Amram holding court down below with a dozen night-groove professionals jammering with flailing arms, and the ceiling puppets dancing their legs and everyone lending a florescent ear.

Amazingly with these kinds of nights, they never end. We fall back into the earthly scene below as the conversation spun around the circle a dozen more times like a roulette wheel landing on different stories in different voices with vibrating laughing on every side until we spun the wheel again and a whole new slice plugged into the center. Zoom, a'la riffin, raffin', Dean and rappin', holy scripture, as Dave leans in and whisper-says — "Well Brian, of all of these shows we've done, (pause) This one was the best." And me just beaming and noddin' and goin' "Yep. That feels right."

And as we're driving home in Dave's superfarmcruiser, I think of Jack in the passenger seat as I study the kinetic driver, pulling out the video camera instead of the nickel notebook, and start filming digital notes of Maestro Dave as we cruised the deserted movie-set-lit 3 A.M. in the universe streets of lower Manhattan, headin' downtown, past the Roman revival courthouses and the towering colonnades of New York City's history, and riding in this all-encompassing good-vibe flow with drummer Deb Reul in the back as we're heading for her friend's palatial downtown spread, I finally break the courage ice and ask Dave for the first time ever, after doing so many shows together for so many years, "Hey

Dave, in what way did tonight evoke what you and Jack did? In what way did we get there?" And he said, in his wonderful poetic rambling but point-driven monologue, "Brian," he paused, "I gotta tell ya . . . this was much nicer than what we did at that time."

2

Hollywood & Sign

When the idea hatched to finally write up some of the Cassady Road Tales, the L.A. half of the 50th anniversary Scroll shows was an obvious must-do. The show was the West Coast mirror of the one done in New York at the start of the month — but this story was written 17 years later.

Event: 50th Anniversary of Jack finishing writing the
       On The Road *scroll*
Date: April 21st – 23rd, 2001
Locations: The Short Stop, Los Angeles; Santa Monica
       Airport; Hollywood Hills; Hollywood sign
Written: May 2018

By the Fates' good graces and to my delight — MTV Networks was flying me out to L.A. to be part of their big Nickelodeon Kid's Choice Awards show in April 2001 — including Sunday the 22nd — the 50th anniversary of the day Jack finished The Scroll.

With that began a whole *other* wild Adventure! And this is where it got really interesting.

As Jack wrote Neal shortly after finishing the 120 feet, he wrote the Scroll "From Apr. 2 to Apr. 22 ...." As soon as I saw the dates in L.A. I thought, "What if I did a show in New York on the day he started it . . . and one in L.A. on the day he finished it?!"

As a New Yorker, I knew how to put together shows here. But I knew enough to know I wasn't on-the-ground enough to do an *On The Road* show out there without some serious local help.

One of the first things I did was get in touch with ol' John Cassady in S.F. We'd just done a few shows together in Amsterdam — in fact, I hosted he & Carolyn's first time ever together on a stage over there around the end of 1999 . . . .

On stage in Amsterdam in 1999
inducting Neal into the Counterculture Hall of Fame.

The Cassadys were inducting Neal, and I Jack, into the Counterculture Hall of Fame there. And I thought, if we're bringing *On The Road* to life on the West Coast, my Beat Brother had to be on stage with me bringing it all home.

He was still workin at some big computer job in Silicon Valley at the time, so he had the dough and the weekends off to be able to make a Sunday, April 22nd show. Boom! One call and done!

So now we had Hassett & Cassady going On The Road . . . coming from New York and San Francisco into —> Target: L.A.

I started calling and emailing around — the latter of which was still relatively new at the dawn of '01. I eventually got a tip — if you wanted to do a Beat show in L.A. — you wanted to talk to S.A.

Griffin, that is.

He and I had been in touch before. A few months earlier, he (along with the now late but always great James Stauffer) had been trying to get me & a bunch of others to come to some massive summit in the Midwest he was working on — The Holy Fools Week – The Big Beat Roadshow Vortex 2000 — in Wichita, Kansas.

Sadly that Super-Summit never materialized, but at least I had the guy's email, and musta had his phone number, too, cuz I called him from MTV due to the time-sensitive nature of the proceedings. When we spoke for the first time, and I told him all about the show, he seemed interested and said he'd get back to me, but then I never heard from him for a week or so. When I called back to see if he'd found a venue, he was like, "Oh, it's you. You were serious about that?"

A few months later when we were reflecting on everything, he told me, "Yeah, I get a lot of people calling me to put on crackpot ideas for shows that never happen. And here was some bozo from the Spice Girls Network saying he wanted to do an *On The Road* show. *Yeah, sure.* I thought about it for about as long as the phone call and that was it."

But I kept on him, as I'm apt to do, and somehow ended up convincing him it was real, and once you do that with ol' S.A. Griffin and he gets a show in his sites, clear the runway!

After our feast in the East, we were gonna have a fest in the West!

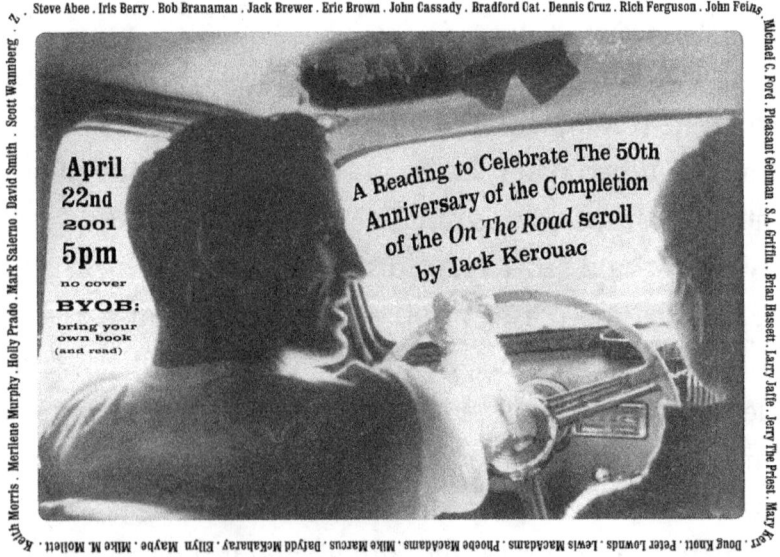

The Short Stop 1455 Sunset Blvd. Los Angeles, CA

Show poster designed by Andy Takakjian.

He ended up finding a Sunset Boulevard bohemian hideaway called the Short Stop that'd been a gangster's speakeasy during prohibition, then a neighborhood beat cop clubhouse ... that we'd convert into a Beat bop clubhouse. He told me about bullet holes in the walls and doors, and old gun lockers, and history of the place doing whatever the hell it wanted. Sounded like our kinda joint.

Then he rounded up a helluva list of L.A. offenders — including the great Lewis MacAdams, a fellow Boulder '82 Jack Super-Summit alumnus and the interviewer in *What Happened To Kerouac?;* founding '50s Beat Bob Branaman; the Beat film documentarian Mary Kerr; his fellow Carma Bums Scott Wannberg, Doug Knott & Mike M Mollett (who founded the L.A. Mudpeople); as well as loads of other top-notch California troublemakers like the proto punks Ellyn Maybe, Iris Berry, Pleasant Gehman, and Black Flag and Circle Jerks co-founder Keith Morris, Michael C. Ford, Rich Ferguson, Bradford Cat, Merilene Murphy (RIP), Jerry the Priest & a whole bunch more.

I flew out a week early to help produce the Kids' Choice Awards, which primarily involved sliming Tom Cruise — so it was all for a noble cause, you understand.

MTV's LA office was of course an ultra-modern architectural masterpiece which thrilled this fan of the medium. And to contrast the very 21st century vibe, the lobby had a massive art installation with an old Airstream trailer and a home "TV room" circa the early 1960s, with the big TV cabinet, TV dinner trays, old curtains & lamps, and it felt like you were walking back in time every time you walked through the lobby. It was really more TV

Land (one of our many other networks) than it was MTV, but I'm a total sucker for that retro stuff.

These were some fairly halcyon days with tons of hit shows across the various networks — MTV had *Unplugged, Real World, Road Rules, Celebrity Deathmatch, The Tom Green Show,* and we were developing *The Osbournes*, which came out the next year and was the biggest ratings hit ever. Our sister network VH1 had *Behind The Music, Storytellers, Legends & Divas*, and Nickelodeon had *Rugrats, Dora The Explorer, SpongeBob SquarePants, Blues Clues* and a ton of others. So we had millions and millions of eyeballs every day from preschoolers to old geezers. In fact, at the time, MTV was in more homes in the world than any other network, including our closest rival, CNN. And it was before the interwebs crashed the advertising biz, so we had a lot of dough and could throw some pretty big parties. Which Kids' Choice largely was.

I was staying over at the fancy Casa Del Mar Spa & Resort right on the ocean, and scammed a second room key for my "assistant" . . . John Cassady.

The awards show itself was held in this enormous all-purpose hangar at the Santa Monica Airport that's used for all kinds of productions — the joint even once housed Howard Hughes' private plane. Rosie O'Donnell hosted, as she often did, and Destiny's Child was the big act of the day — before Beyoncé left to take over the world. The event's known for dousing celebrities in the network's trademark green slime, and at this show even a good portion of the audience got it as well, which of course they loved, cuz what kid doesn't love green slime?

The whole endeavor is kind of pointless and self-serving if you wanna know the truth, but then that's probably the case with all these Hollywood award shows. And as is probably also always the case, the after-party was when the real fun started. We had one separate area for all the kids and their parents, and then a whole huge adult / celebrity party zone where there were potted palm trees and all sorts of little silk-walled nooks and open bars and people like Halle Berry and Jessica Simpson and that *Dawson's Creek* guy, and I don't know if they were in the bar area or not but Mila Kunis and Lil Bow Wow and the *Malcom In The Middle* kid and a bunch of others were running around among all the hip suits and tight dresses.

Johnny found himself a spot he liked to stand, and hung there by the hour with a big Cheshire grin taking in all the babes and hijinx while I zipped around the party fulla colleagues and newbees, and kept circling back to him, who didn't really want to budge from his beatific bliss.

One of the times I came looping back he was talking to some cute young California brunette, and they were both smiling uncommonly wide. "Hey!"

"This is Aurora," he told me. "She's an English major and she's actually heard of those beatnik bums," he said with a laugh.

"Oh, nice!" I said, shaking her hand. "How did you come to be at this little shindig?"

"My dad's the production manager. He does a lot

of shows here," she said with that casually blasé seen-it-all-before L.A. vibe.

"Nice. So . . . you're an English major?"

"Yeah, I'm getting my Masters at UCLA. It's alright. I'm studying literary journalism, mainly Joan Didion and Martha Gellhorn at the moment. She just died recently. Of course I read the Tom Wolfe book about this guy's Dad and his friends," as she flipped her thumb mock dismissively towards John.

"And I guess Hunter Thompson," I tossed.

"Oh yeah, of course. And Mailer and Capote and Orwell and Twain's reportage and ..."

"All the usual suspects," John chimed in with one of his stock lines and laughed because he finds just about everything funny.

"I loved *Slouching Toward Bethlehem* and *The White Album*," I said to her Joan Didion mention. "I wish more women wrote like that."

"Yeah, so do I," she said.

"Did John tell you about the show we're doin tomorrow?"

"*No,*" she said, with a heavy stress on the italics of it all.

"Oh yeah," he burst with a laugh.

"It was 50 years ago tomorrow that Kerouac finished writing the Scroll of *On The Road* — and that's pretty close to literary nonfiction."

"*Really!* You're doing a show? And didn't mention it?" as she looked at John with playful suspicion.

"Oh no, I was getting right to that. It was the very

next thing," he assured her, and I laughed at how much he was like his Dad around women.

"You get on that, Cassady. I'm gonna keep making the rounds," I told them, happy John had somebody gorgeous to talk to.

"Nice to meet you," I said to her.

"Yes, you too," as she stuck out her dainty hand and flashed that wide white-teethed million-dollar California smile.

"That damn Cassady," I'm thinking as I walked away. "I'm working the room all day trying to make some kind of headway, and he just stands there doin nuthin' and ends up with a babe. Fucker."

I dove back into the now well-lubricated news and ad sales krewe I knew from New York, and with the main event behind us and everything a success it was approaching off-the-clock time in lovely downtown L.A. on a Saturday night. Everybody was in a high mood. Rosie O'Donnell came out and did a bit of a schmooze, very gregarious and a real people-person type of person. Never saw the big movie star Tom Cruise anywhere, but Rosie was out posing for pictures and laughing loudly and hugging people and generally causing a scene, so much so she reminded me of Edie Kerouac. Neither were petit birds, nor reserved and quiet like, say, Carolyn Cassady, but both rather boisterous and quite comfortable being the center of attention and stirring the drink.

Within the world of MTV Networks, little known fact, and don't spread this around, but although the ad sales people actually wore suits and the women fancy clothes (unlike everyone else in the massive casual company), they partied harder than any other department I ever came in contact with. So I was right at home.

"Brian! You're in L.A.! We gotta show you a good time," one of them assured me as I rejoined the fray.

"Aren't you doing some show out here? You just did one in New York, right?" asked another.

"Yeah," and I told them about the 50th anniversary and all that, and they were all genuinely enthusiastic about it, but I was pretty sure I wouldn't be seeing any of them at the old speakeasy full of beatniks tomorrow.

"You should check the schedule for the Hollywood Bowl," the most music-centric suggested. "I don't know how long you're here, but if you can catch a show there you'd be really glad you did."

"Boy, I'd *love* to. It seems like Red Rocks West," I said, and a couple of them actually got it.

"Have you ever heard of the Watts Towers?" another asked.

"Oh my God — yeah! Right!" I blurted. "That's here! Shit — I gotta get there! That's why Jerry Garcia formed the Grateful Dead cuz of those towers."

"What? I thought that was in San Francisco he did that."

"No — it was here. It was the Watts Towers," I said, getting all incoherently excited. "It was after the Watts Acid Test in '66, and he was driving back home after the gig with Neal Cassady — the central guy in *On*

The Road that we're celebrating tomorrow — and he had this profound moment where he'd been fluctuating between whether he should be a solo artist like a painter, which he also was besides being a musician, and which he saw Neal as, and the guy who made the Watts Towers, which was specifically his reference thought — or if he should be in a group collaboration, like the rock band he was starting — he was at this fork in the road in the car with Cassady — and that night he decided to go with the rock group ... and the rest is history."

"You should be writing our *Behind The Music*s, you're a walking encyclopedia on this shit," one of them said with a smile.

"Speaking of art, you gotta get to the Getty," another suggested, knowing I was that way inclined. "Besides all the art, just the views and the gardens and the building are to die for."

"Thanks! What's the view like from the Hollywood sign?" I asked, and they laughed.

"I'm sure it's great, but you can't go there. It's not open to the public or anything," I was duly advised.

Although they knew of my art proclivities, apparently my Prankster background had eluded them.

And we kept jamming all sorts of ideas and industry gossip & such including how Beyoncé was going to go solo soon and be a huge star, and as things were kind of winding down, the musical guy I liked the best said, "A couple of us are going to a party up in the hills. You should come."

"Well, that sounds perfect. I got a show tomorrow,

but it's not 'til 5," and off we were on the next Adventure.

I circled back to grab Cassady . . . but I came across an empty space! I trembled and explored but there was nuthin' in his place. The phone came out and I got on, that's when it all began — there was Cowboy John and he was gone in the car to hippie Venice-land.

"We're heading to Venice Beach," he told me. "She says there's some bookstore there I have to check out. What's it called again?" he asked her. "Oh yeah. Beyond Baroque."

"Well, don't be late for breakfast. Or at least lunch. We got a big show tomorrow," I reminded the Casanova of California.

"Uncle Jack's big day. I wouldn't miss it," he assured me from a speeding car headed in the opposite direction.

One Cassady down, one party up. In the hills that is. Swimming pools, movie stars. Literally, in the Hollywood Hills. Which is actually a place, where there's actually hills. Manhattan this ain't.

I followed the lead car, crossing Wilshire Boulevard, Santa Monica Boulevard, Sunset Boulevard, Hollywood Boulevard . . . all these places I'd heard about all my life in songs and movies and TV shows . . . and suddenly they were peopled by real people . . . who actually *lived* here. *Who does that?!*

Eventually we were winding up this steep narrow barely-two-lane road, weaving around tight corners with tall solid fence walls built right to the edge of the road like we were in a maze without an inch to spare. And suddenly homeboy slowed down and turned through the narrow unmarked gateway of a ten-foot-high fence into the courtyard of a dream. There was a fountain in the middle of a round driveway, but of course almost nowhere to park — apparently a bunch of people were here already. And I got my first sense of the car-envy status-symbol culture of L.A. where everybody has a Beemer or Mercedes or snazzy retro convertible with the top left down because it never rains in Southern California.

It was the home of some big ad exec, and everything looked perfect like it was staged for a magazine or a movie or something. *Do people really* <u>live</u> *like this?!* There was enough space to play ball hockey in the foyer! But it was a bit too nice of course, with marble everything, and floor-to-ceiling windows looking out over the flickering lights of the city, and walls covered with big colorful Hockneys and Jim Dines and Peter Maxes, and a baby grand piano in the corner, with this really open plan where there was only a hint of a wall separating the giant white plushy living room from the massive darker kitchen / dining / party room, with a sliding glass wall that was mostly open leading out to the obligatory swimming pool that had a whole marble terrace around it with all sorts of rich green plants framing the perimeter.

I was clearly the lowest roller in this highfalutin' scene. And the least manicured. And least tailored. And obviously the guy from outta town and outta the loop. But once I was introduced around, they were pretty friendly and actually seemed to kind of be embracing a non-player in their game.

I knew a couple of the 20 or so people from the extended MTV family, and one of them, as soon as he saw me, said, "Hey Brian! C'mere, I got something for you," and walked me out to the flickering nocturnal pool and tiki torch patio. "Here," and he hands me a little pink ecstasy pill. They're all into feeling good all the time in California, and who was I to argue.

After that, things got rather warm & fuzzy rather quickly.

The swimming pool was twinkling and the grand piano tinkling and everyone was drinking and thinking about everything that was happening. There was a magician comedian coughing cards out his mouth, and gold sequined dresses worn as comfortably as jeans & a t-shirt, and everyone was so refined and pretty, yet debauched and decadent. I've hung with primo beatniks and hippies, but these guys were smokin' even better weed ... in even fatter joints ... with an even better view.

And a few of them were actually really interested in the whole Kerouac *On The Road* scroll story. They couldn't believe it. And that was one of many interesting things — that this was not at all in their wheelhouse, but they totally got it when I explained the significance of this guy writing his book in 20 days that changed history. And we were all just a month away from the sacred Scroll going to auction and being bought by one of these rich cool people. They *do* exist! [Check the full auction story coming next in this book!]

And this being Hollywood, they were interested

in why it hadn't been made into a movie yet ... and I gave then the whole Francis Ford Coppola backstory as it stood in 2001 — not knowing 10 years later it would finally get made . . . and I'd fall in with the director and have a hundred Adventures on that front. [See also *How The Beats Begat The Pranksters* book, and the *On The Road to The Hall Of Fame* story a little later in this book!]

With the handful I had captivated with all this stuff, I mentioned the show tomorrow, and they were like, "Well, what is it you *do?*"

Anybody who knows me, knows I've been carrying a sidebag on me since frickin' high school, so of course I had the scripts for tomorrow's show with me, and right there with the California breeze blowing through the kitchen of this mansion on the hill, I read the end of *On The Road* to this bunch of receptive ears with open eyes, growing smiles and raging dopamine. It was suddenly Jack — live and in the air — the words he wrote 50 years ago this very weekend — echoing through eternity — through the mansions of money he never hit — to ears he never met — the chorus of his song playing to the star-maker machinery in the 21st century.

The host was playing some new cartoon movie that was gonna be released next month in his home screening theater, but of course I had no interest and wanted to talk to the babes and dig the view and snort the lines of this partying krewe. At some point about a dozen people I hadn't seen before suddenly appeared and were raving about this animated thing with Eddie Murphy and Mike Meyers called *Shrek*.

It was general mayhem for generous hours in this palace of pleasures, and at one point in the ecstasy of the ecstasy I realized — I was in the Hollywood Hills! The Hollywood sign!! Ah Yes!

Talk to people — figure it out. I do — and I did. Got directions from out the front gate. Just a little zip-a-dee-doo-dah here and there, and Bob Hope's your uncle, you're there! One of the actors on the patio playground — Mario — still remember his name — the guy with the key sacred tip — told me in the daylight you could see a path up, basically under the "D." Ahhh ... copy that.

Knowing I had a show tomorrow and a tip tonight, I made a relatively early exit from a party I assume is still going on — but it was time to hit The Road . . . on the weekend of Jack.

Back in the spaceship, Han Solo at the wheel of a Neal to another deal — gotta prank it, gotta make it — gotta find the way.

Vacant streets in vacant hills of voluptuous hoods. Everybody's already where they're gonna be, and it's just me, in a mischievous mousetrap maze of madness, muddling my way to the top of the hill. "If the road's going *up* I'm going in the right direction." Get to the top. Get to the top. There's gotta be a way.

Couldn't believe it, but I wove all the right weaves, and maneuvered myself to the peak point of civilization just south of the horizontal beaming white American monolith.

Back behind the last house on the last street there was a little narrow cement driveway-type road that looked like it was leading to the peak! And the chain that stretched across blocking it . . . *was lying on the ground!*

DONE!

But there was no damn way with the cops' ways these days I was gonna run some Hunter Thompson play on this mad Saturday . . . but I knew I'd found the way.

And tomorrow was SUNDAY SUNDAY SUNDAY !

In super sunny surreal L.A.!

I gotta slay!

Can't burn the day

on a jailhouse play.

Back home to stay I gotta sway.

Jack's Scroll birth we gotta lay.

= * = * = * = * = * = * = * = * =

Waking up on that momentous Sunday, April 22nd — a Sunday just as it was in 1951 — the wondrous day Jack reached the end of his long scroll *Road* on the tracing paper parchment — the ending that Lucien Carr's dog Potchky would later chew up — the climax of his singular 20-day streak that, as he told his brother Neal in a letter a couple months later, **"I wrote that book on COFFEE ... remember said rule. Benny, tea, anything I know none as good as coffee for real mental power kicks. . . . Remember! COFFEE! (try it, please.)"**

I felt just as buzzed as Jack prolly did on this buzzing day.

His Cassady was on the other side of the continent on this morning in 1951. Mine was on the other side of town. God knows where, but surely with the Aurora of the dawn, after the cumming of complete night that blesses the earth, as Jack wrote this day in the final paragraph of the book that finally pushed him into the global spotlight.

It was also Earth Day, April 22nd, following the biggest one ever in 2000, and it's also my Mother's birthday! God bless her, an environmentalist before there was a word for it. But THIS April 22nd in 1951, as Jack recounted in another letter to Neal, he wrote an astounding 15,000 words in one day to bring it home!

And now we were gonna bring *him* home to this railroad earth — with a cast of thousands — or at least a couple hundred — to elevate the Pentagon — or raise the dead on this 50th Pentecost year and share His Light with all the peoples of the world. Or at least Echo Park.

I arrived at the Short Stop speakeasy well before showtime and it was already a chaotic circus of crazy creatives carving up the scenery, led by the director of today's movie, S.A. Griffin.

Amazingly, he'd had a shirt made emblazoned with the classic *OTR* line about "... the mad ones ... DESIROUS of Everything AT THE SAME TIME ..." written in creative font-smashing text covering his chest — broadcasting its meaningful message in a playful style, perfectly reflecting his prankster essence.

The club was already a buzzing hive full of L.A. actors and poets and show people decorating the large performance space with bodies and actions — a room that looked like a fancy Goodfellas' lounge from the '50s or '60s with almost no lighting so the celebrities and gangsters and cops could discreetly entertain in deep red vinyl booths surrounding the open dance floor in the middle — the only lighting being flickering candles in large red-tinted translucent holders on every table as well as lining the perimeter of the stage.

In the middle of the dance floor lay a giant 3-foot-by-4-foot print of the first part of The Scroll — and scattered all around it like fallen leafs were page leafs of *On The Road* that throughout the celebration people would pick up any random one and read it from the stage, a la Burroughs' cut-up method, except whole pages to collage the poetry of the prose into a swirl of images and passages and dialog and details jumbled together proving how powerful and consistent the wordsmithing was that you could hear chapter 1 or 51 and it would still fit together like a matching set.

S.A. created something I've never experienced at any Jack show before or since — a massive mad celebratory krewe of joyous orgasmicly LOUD participatory audience-performer-melding dancing dingledodies — AND I mean, LOUD! It was MAD high energy at 6PM on a Sunday like it was a midnight on a Saturday at Mardi Gras.

The room became more than packed. The pages on

the dance floor were soon blown up to the lip of the stage as the place lifted up with men & women floor-dancing in floor-sitting crosslegged positions, the doorways crammed with faces peering in.

And like the rock star he was, Cassady came strolling in just before showtime with his latest babe on his arm and perpetual smile on his face. He was laughing and she was beaming and the party was screaming and I thought I was dreaming.

Happy J.C. in Venice Beach.

From the moment S.A. stepped to the microphone
to open it — and he's one guy who doesn't even *need* a
microphone to fill a room with his booming performer's
voice — the souls he'd assembled soared and roared like
an arena rock show.

I kicked it off with the beginning of the original
Scroll text that I'd acquired through a connection who'd
transcribed it from the only two photographs of it that
had been published as of 2001, and right from the first
line people were Howling "Go!" ... "Yeah!" ... "Wow!"
and laughing and cheering. And the next readers
began improvising off-script and working the room,
the audience riffling in lines in harmony with Jack's in
a collective kaleidoscopic recreation of the creation of
the Beats. As loud and orgasmic as new life comes! with
beaming faces and embracing hugs and love and sweat
and knowing twinkles between bubbling souls.

There were no rehearsals, no memorized scripts,
just the chaos of people running to the microphone with
parts of the Scroll or part of the Book in what S.A. coined
"Bop Bingo!" With madmen yelling "Go Go Go!" from the
swirling booths, S.A. copped "the mad ones" line in this
mad hang-out as it blazed from his chest in case anyone
missed the obvious.

Then one of his crazy Carma Bums co-conspirators,
the now late-great Scott Wannberg, stepped up to speed-
read Jack at the tempo he probably typed, causing even
faster "Go"s from all over the room.

Then Michael C. Ford drove into the spotlight all
high-energy — the Grammy-nominated spoken-word

artist who performed with Jim Morrison back in the L.A. day, and recorded with all the other Doors since — he took the wild Slim Gaillard club show part of *On The Road* out for a playful right-orooni ride, getting all Putti-Putti all-rooti, as the audience started laughing-orooni with all the be-bop-orooni a-la-vooni shim-sham jimmy-jam thank-you-man howdy-doody, all-rooti! The room was howling and the stage raging and spirits dancing and Jack's typewriter clacking a thousand miles an hour as the high-powered Ford fired on all cylinders to crack the code and break the barrier and spike the sound and remind us all that — "To Slim Gaillard the whole world was just one big orooni!"

Then John and I took the stage, the Bebop Brothers flip the page, bringing back the driving sage, pinning needles on the gauge.

Johnny riffed how his Dad was just a big grown up kid, and how he'd come home and be fun and funny as hell, often bringing strange gifts, like a little hollow wooden pig he brought back from Mexico that if you put a live fly inside it, would actually cause it to walk across the table. (!)

And how he loved his Dad, and even if other people claimed Neal was off having Adventures with them, it felt to John like Dad was home all the time. And how his Mom had to be the disciplinarian, and how he grew up with a fairly idyllic childhood — one parent providing the roof over head and meals on the table, and the other being a big adventure buddy.

And we traded off *On The Road* readings, John

partial to the jazz joint riffs, punctuating them with personalized details and comedic asides. "Everybody was rocking and roaring," he read. "'Galatea and Marie with beer in hands were standing on their chairs, shaking and jumping.' — What a party! Where was I?!"

And every time Jack would quote his Dad yelling, "Whoo!" or "Go!" to the jazz, the audience would yell it back to John creating a call-and-response song out of a prose-and-participate book.

And sitting right in the front was a gorgeous cross-legged L.A. woman dancing from the waist up, arms flowing in hypnotic figure-eights, fingers snapping … then exploding like slow-motion fireworks, all in an above-waist interpretive dance — part sign language, part snake-charming seduction.

And Sugar Magnolia, as I took to calling Aurora, was half the time on the side of the stage, half the time against a wall in the light in our joyous view, and half the time at one of the tables taking notes.

And John & I hit The Road together — reading the Jack & Neal car-riding "IT" section from *On The Road* that George Walker & I would later appropriate and open every one of our 20 shows together 20 years later, but this was the first time either John or I ever duetted it, and he had the Neal rhythms *down*. Naturally.

"… everybody knows it's not the tune that counts — but IT!"

And speaking of tunes, the most musical of all the Cassadys, Johnny C. Goode, broke out his electric guitar and filled in the colors with "minor love key progressions" as he called it while I read the part of *On The Road* after his Dad dropped off Uncle Jack in the California sister city of San Francisco and he started to have hunger-induced hallucinations. "I had reached the point of ecstasy that I always wanted to reach, which was the complete step across chronological time into timeless shadows, and wonderment in the bleakness of the mortal realm ..." as Johnny accented the "wonderment" with his crystalline lines.

And with the Ken Burns' *Jazz* series having just aired on PBS, we thought we'd offer up Jack's own history of jazz in one of the *OTR* riffs that Amram remembered as one of Jack's favorites that he liked to read aloud — the "children of the American bop night" paragraph that begins, "Once there was Louis Armstrong blowing his beautiful top in the muds of New Orleans ..." where he lays out the whole evolutionary tale in one page that Ken Burns took 20 hours to tell.

And Johnny picked up on the *Johnny B. Goode* echoes when Jack wrote of "Charlie Parker, a kid in his mother's woodshed in Kansas City, blowing his taped-up alto among the logs, practicing on rainy days" and how that was captured so similarly by Maestro Chuck — "Way back up in the woods behind the evergreens, There stood a log cabin made of earth and wood . . . He used to carry his guitar in a gunny sack, Go sit beneath the tree by the railroad track," as John melded Bird and Berry into a single rockin Bebop-a-Lula, and oh boy that little country boy could play!

Ragtime became Swing became Big Band became

Bop became Rock n Roll became the Acid Tests became Woodstock became a million bands that burned burned burned like fabulous roman candles across the land.

Then John & I took a trip "to see George Shearing at Birdland in the midst of the long, mad weekend," as Jack opened another of his favorite *On The Road* passages that he read to Amram's backup back in the day, now with a Cassady in on the tune, and Johnny warmed up, effortlessly pealing off riffs, "slowly at first, then the beat went up, and he began rocking fast, his left foot jumped up with every beat … his combed hair dissolved and he began to sweat!"

The audience was now howling like a collective mad Moriarty yelling for us to "GO!!" as Cassady soared and the audience roared with every new chord that felt like a sword pulled from a stone! Excalibur!

"There he is! That's him! Oh God, Oh God, Cassady, Yes! Yes! Yes!" And Johnny was conscious of the madmen in front of him, he could hear every one of their gasps and imprecations!

"That's right!" they said. "Yeesssssss!"

And then Bradford Cat sidled up, the hip wing of the famous Bancroft family of California and Tom Hanks' wild friend in *Bachelor Party*, who read the *OTR* part about Neal nearly driving into the truck on the bridge, and John kept playing beside him, driving that train, high on the vein, of the family's Road bane — the ever insane

Neal at the wheel.

And the next guy flowed in riffing the Three Stooges-like Henri Cru / Remi Boncoeur part about the two of them hopelessly haplessly stealing boxes of food from the construction worker barracks in Marin — happily sparking my old pal Henri back to life in Los Angeles in the 21st century — refraining his classic comedic derangements about their pilfering life, like, "You know what President Truman said. 'We must cut down on the cost of living.'"

And at some point John wandered back into the microphone mix, telling the story he'd later write up in his *Visions of Neal* book about when he was 12 years old and he and his friends would "borrow" the neighborhood rich kid's motor-less go-kart to take rides down the roads of the foothills of the Santa Cruz Mountains where they lived. After telling his Dad about it, Neal asked if he could do it with them, and John, caught by surprise, said "Sure!"

They went over the next morning but the family was out, and Neal said, "Oh well, maybe another time," but John convinced him that they had permission to borrow it, "a complete and utter fabrication," as John puts it. Neal squeezed into the little car like a clown at the circus with his elbows and knees comically sticking out but grinning from ear-to-ear as they took the kart for several spins down the hill. It was all a fun & games until ... the owners' car appeared at the top of the rise. Doh! Not only were the kids caught red-handed, but one of their fathers was in on it!! And there was Neal, hanging his head in shame, caught with his hand in the go-kart jar, shuffling his feet and trying to stammer some excuse, when of course there was none — save Neal's penchant for Adventures in other people's cars.

And we peaked out the show with S.A. reading the climax of *On The Road* — then handing the book to John to deliver the eternal benediction, "I think of Dean Moriarty, I even think of the old Dean Moriarty the father we never found, I think of Dean Moriarty."

It was a beautiful, Perfect Moment — John's voice bringing to life Jack's lament to his fallen father on the 50th anniversary of the very day he wrote those very words.

Yes yes yes.

= * = * = * = * = * = * = * = * =

The next morning we woke up to the clearest day in L.A. history. Or so it seemed. And we could see the Hollywood sign clear from our window in Santa Monica. Or so it seemed. But . . . ah-ha!!

Mission On! Show behind us. One last day to make our play. After the gig with a roomful of L.A.'s kindest, we were sufficiently supplied with gifts of muggles, or "Elitch" as Jack & Neal sometimes referred in code to their sacred herbs (named for the botanical garden in Denver where they used to sneak off and smoke it), and us both being adults of the adult beverage variety, we stopped at the colorful corner gated war-torn variety store and loaded up on cold Heinekens for a healthy day's Prank.

As we drove through the now-familiar streets and sites of the shining city under an uncommonly blue-sky day, I kept singing Randy Newman's *I Looooove L.A.* — prompting John to chime in every time with the song's non-musical refrain — "We love it!" and then laugh.

He kept breaking into his schmaltzy schtick version of, *Hoo-ray for Hollywood,* making up crazy lyrics about whatever he saw out the windows and doing a little chorus line dance with his hands.

I had a bona fide folded paper map, and Johnny was the navigator, and we expeditiously zoomed ourselves to the base of Beachwood Drive, which seemed to be the spine of Hollywoodland — and as soon as we turned onto it — BOOM! There was the sign blazing right in front of us!! And John immediately started snapping pictures!

My notes from a couple nights ago told me to stay on Beachwood up the curlicue winding hill road and find Ledgewood Drive. These hills were *so much different* — and better — in the daylight! I could see more than headlit fences — old fashioned street lamps, and all these gorgeous strange homes squeezed together and perched on the most precarious of cliff protrusions — Spanish, modern, round houses, A-frames, rectangle ones that looked like mobile homes. A lot of the properties and houses were surprisingly small — almost like glorified cottages, which I later found out some of them actually were!

"Choice real estate," John dryly played. "Boy, it's quiet. I could be comfortable up here. . . . . . . Century 21 . . . I'll take it."

"Somebody was telling me at that party the other night that you could still get a place here for less than a gazillion dollars as recently as the '70s!"

"You're kidding! . . . Who knew?!" John laughed. Then he slowed down, thoughtfully, slowly, reverentially whispering, "Man, there musta been *some kinda parties* in these joints!" as he spun his head up down and all around.

Then some driving school student & teacher came down the narrow winding hill toward us. "Driving school?!" John burst! *"Don't bring her up here* — what, are you nuts?!"

"Apparently Aldous Huxley lived here for a while," I shared. "I guess a lot of people did, but that's one guy I'd love to have hung with at his house."

"Walked through his Doors of Perception," John said laughing at himself. "I dig it. . . . . The Doors — that's another L.A. band." And he turned on his thick faux Beatles accent — "That's where they got their name, you know."

He craned his head some more. "Rockcliff Drive — gee, where'd they get that name?"

Then all of a sudden — "There's the sign! Bigger than snot!" John blurted as soon as we found ourselves nearly underneath it.

We came up to some road with a "DO NOT ENTER — PRIVATE LANE" sign that we knew to ignore without hesitation. "We're coming to visit my rich uncle," John started running through his excuse lines in case we needed them.

We wove around the nearly one-lane streets until we got to the very last house with the even smaller road to the top right behind it and — *WHOA! Screech!* The chain was *up!!* The hidden secret sure-thing road I'd just scouted not 48 hours earlier . . . now had the chain across!! Uuuuuuugh!

And right there on the side of the road was an official city street sign with big red letters — "NO HIKING ALLOWED TO HOLLYWOOD SIGN." Aaaaaahhhhhh!!!

"Oh well," John says, as in, "We gave it a shot." To which I responded by looking for a parking spot.

Which there were NONE of anywhere up there because everybody's fences came right up to the edge of the properties along the barely-2-cars-can-squeeze-by-each-other road. "You couldn't park *a bike* up here," I said looking everywhere. Of course, I'd done no pre-scout on *parking* cuz it looked like we could drive right up!

Finally we found a sort-of space by an intersection where we could just barely squeeze off the road and two cars could still get by.

And as soon as we got out, as John had noticed earlier, it was *dead quiet* — except for tons of birds chirping. There were very few houses to begin with, and they were probably all owned by people off making money to afford them, and besides, we were right on the edge of the ginormous parkland that was The Hollywood Hill with The Sign.

Of course I begin a very thorough day-packing including the video camera and copious beers and all the other supplies for a day-long Adventure Picnic. And John's all Cassady-like antsy, shuffling his feet in the railroad earth, hemmin' and hawin' about we better get goin' already. "Get this show On The Road."

But I knew the afternoon I was packing for and didn't want to forget anything.

Eventually we hiked back up the road to below the "D" — and sure as shootin' — *there's the trail.* But there was also this giant BILLBOARD of a sign — with massive lettering of massive warnings — 'THERE IS NO CLIMBING OR ACCESS TO THE HOLLYWOOD SIGN" — then ... pursuant to all these laws and how much the fines were — all as official and off-putting as they could possibly put it.

And John was looking at it . . . "Oh well, we got close. This is good," and starts snapping pictures of the big sign up the hill. And I'm looking at him like he's nuts, thinking, "If you think there's any way that billboard is stopping us, you're crazier than I know you are."

I started pulling out every line in the book: "They don't mean it" . . . "We're just tourists" . . . "We're not actually going to *do* anything wrong" . . . "The L.A.P.D. have more to do than chase down kids at a sign" . . . "We only live once" . . . "We're here" . . . .

"Yeaaaaah . . . . I dunno," John said, completely unconvinced. "I'm gettin too old for this shit." But I knew there was *no god-damned way* I was gonna get this close and not get up there. I was about ready to tell him he could go back and wait in the car cuz I wuz going up. In fact I might've even said something like that. But I remember what worked.

Woody freakin' Guthrie!

God bless 'im!

I thought, if I could just get John looking at *the back* of that sign and not the front . . . .

So I started singing *This Land Is Your Land.* [Tip from your Uncle Bri: If you wanna get to a musician's brain — go through his musical heart.]

In particular the verse —

"As I went walking, I saw a sign there,
And on the sign said, 'No Trespassing.'
But on the other side – it didn't say nothing,
That side was made for you and me."

"Look," and I pointed to a nearby natural desert hillock — almost a mini "scenic overlook" — about a hundred feet up beyond the sign. "Let's just go there and see how we feel. We'll know right away if sirens go off or the dogs are unleashed or whatever. And at least we'll get a better view from there without this stupid sign in the way."

And somehow . . . . . . that worked!

"Baby Steps, Bob. It's just right there . . . ," I said to close the deal, pointing to the warm-looking beige sitting-hump. "We're not going to the Hollywood Sign if we go there. They don't say anything about you can't go to that little outcrop." And I knew I was gettin through to the old boy. "Let's just go there . . . " and I started walking towards it — and damn if ol' Johnny didn't follow!

BOOM!

There we were in the aromatic spring of a California desert chaparral surrounded by pale coastal scrub, sagebrush and ragweed — prompting us to smoke some fresh California weed we'd ragged from the show. Johnny doesn't actually puff the stuff anymore, but he quite enjoys the smell and celebratory sage burningness of the ritual.

"I remember the first time we got some when I was about 14, and we smoked it in my friend Jim's tree fort," he told me. "The first time I smelled it — Doh! — So *that's* what Dad was smoking all this time! It wasn't Turkish tobacco at all! I felt so uncool for not knowing earlier. But now everything made sense!" and he laughed at his own memories.

Surrounding us were soft desert pastels, and right past our resting feet was a forest of different shades of green trees like a waving real-life Van Gogh in front of us . . . and sharp-roofed houses with manicured lawns in a splay of rich deep colors . . . as we sat like Indians in nature looking at the white man's encroachment. And in that moment both worlds seemed equally beautiful in their own way.

Somehow in the ease of us looking at the beautiful scenery on this beautiful day in this beautiful natural parkland . . . it became obvious we should maybe walk up just a little more. Don't have to go all the way, you understand. "However far we go . . . we could just get a smidge closer." (hee-hee)

And as we followed the "D" path up, the ridge spine we were ascending suddenly narrowed into this little 6-inch-wide mini ridge peak like a natural 15 foot long tightrope in the mountains you had to walk across to make it to the promised land. Dropping down both sides were steep ridge cliffs that went a looooooong way down . . . and were carpeted with these hideous ominous black razor-branched thickets that would slice you up like a machine if you tumbled down.

At some point the city or somebody installed fence posts and barbed wire to close off this necessary natural bridge to reach the sign summit — there was no other way up from the south side (the side you always see it from that faces the sign) if you couldn't cross this treacherous natural divide. But intrepid travelers before us had beaten the thing down, so by the time we got there you could just step over it — the remnants of the last ditch defenses — wooden fence posts and wire like the Wild West days befitting the rugged peopleless empty wind-swept Western desert terrain we were traversing.

We made it over untipsily, and as we stopped to look back — the landscape was just spectacular! — tight little ridges and valleys like a miniature Rocky Mountains, with occasional dense trees that looked like giant bonsai, all in the untouched ruggedness of the Santa Monica Range — on this sunny April day filled with light green spring buds flourishing on the thick covering of desert foliage, all set against a beautiful light beige sandy backdrop.

The last part of the hike became really steep —
some bona fide mountain climbing like Jack & Gary
Snyder in *The Dharma Bums* — now Cassady & Hassett
following in their premonition footsteps up a West Coast
mountain to the north of a major California city in search
of their own satori.

I reached the sign with my youthful New York City
walking legs some good minutes before Uncle John's
bent their way up, and I found a nice rock throne perch
to sit on and crack the first celebratory beer, watching my
brother heave himself up God's staircase until he made
one final lunge with both hands outstretched and grabbed
the steel girder beneath the "D" with the joy of someone
breaking the tape at the end of a marathon.

"GOTCHA!" he exclaimed as soon as he grabbed it.
Then he just hung there, with one hand gripping it and
one hand waving free, swinging around to appreciate the
mountain he'd just conquered. "The Los Angeles basin,"
he gasped between breaths with surveying awe. "Never
seen so much of it at once before."

After he got rested up, he began coveting my cold
bevy relaxation, and made his way up the final steps so
we could move into our new "HOLLYWOOD" apartment
for the day. "I don't want to buy it, I just want to rent it
for an hour or two," I sang to John from the appropriate
Robert Hunter / Jerry Garcia late classic *West L.A.
Fadeaway.*

The first "O" became our hidden basecamp living
room to stash supplies and branch out for short hikes all

around us. It was perfect because you could kind of hide behind it, but also see out the two slanted sides real easy.

"'I'll take an 'O', Pat.' . . . 'There are *three* Os.'"

We had our way with that sign all afternoon with our bagful of cold Heinies and pocketful of pre-rolled bombers. There were hawks and crows and all sorts of birds keeping us company, dancing in the airstream of the mountainside, not unlike ourselves. Bright orange California poppies and deep Van Gogh yellow desert-marigolds filled the flora floor in every direction. The Griffith Observatory was looming large off to the left, and of course I can't look at that without thinking of the classic knife fight scene in Nicholas Ray's *Rebel Without A Cause*, the widow of whom was the first person I ever lived with in New York City in their props-filled loft in SoHo. The giant Hollywood Reservoir lake was right below us, and just beyond that was a clear view into the Hollywood Bowl. And back in his thick Ringo accent, John reminded me, "The Beatles played there you know."

All the seats were pointing right towards us, so this big sign would be directly above the stage for every performance ever laid down there. And we could also see clear as the clear day the classic round stack-of-records Capitol Records building. "Geez, they didn't have far to go from their office to the gig!" my Beatle bud observed. "I read every book about them. Brian Epstein carried the cash from the gigs around in a paper bag. It was so old school / off the charts Bonnie & Clyde in those days," and he laughed at his own memory-thoughts.

Johnny was also the first to spot the construction

workers' names soldered into one of the foundation pillars. "I can't believe this place hasn't had the shit tagged out of it," he said of the graffiti we saw all over L.A. but not up here. "It's a steep hike, though — keeps the riffraff out."

He wanted to go and find Douglas Fairbanks and Mary Pickford's Pickfair house. "But that's in Beverly Hills," he said, pointing with his thumb behind us and once again surprising me with all the details stored on his hard drive. "I love the '20s Hollywood glamor," he said. "Fairbanks was the swashbuckling leading man of the time, and she was a knock-out doll."

"She's Canadian," I told him.

"Really?! Well, nobody's perfect."

"Man, this would be a great place to bring your babe, though, eh?" I said. "Imagine all the wild sex that's gone on up here over the last hundred years!"

"No kidding," John said, then started singing, "I wish they all could be California girrrrls ...."

We went and explored the steep rocky trail up behind the sign that led to a fenced off road at the summit that led to a weather station and cluster of satellite dishes & all sorts of ominous electronic stuff. There were a bunch more "DO NOT ENTER" signs . . . but also a pushed-up gap under one part of the chain-link fence big enough for Yogi Bear to shimmy underneath.

And just as we were coming down from there — we heard the chopper! The fuckin cops were coming!! *"Oh no!"*

"Get behind the 'L'!" I yelled, and I've never seen

ol' Johnny move so fast! Scamper scamper like rabbits from a fox, as we're simultaneously craning our heads all around. Is it above us? Behind us? In front of us? Where the hell is it? It was loud as anything — like it was right on top of our heads!

Out of breath and finally out of luck, we ran to the "L" part where the sign touched the ground so they couldn't see our feet below it. Louder and louder it got — louder and louder that's all! I got down on my knees and prayed. Okay, not so much pray really as poke my head out under a spot of the sign to see what the hell was happening. "God! It's hovering right there!!" as I quickly pulled my eyes back in, waiting for the bullhorn: "Hey you kids! Get out of that Jello tree!"

"What the hell are they doing up here?" my internal monolog said out loud.

"We're in Dutch now," John warned me.

Then it finally started to pull away without seeming to do anything, and we thought we were in the clear, but it quickly circled back and resumed hovering right in front of us . . . . aaaaaaa.

"Oh no! What *now?!*"

And after a while of this non-bullhorn hovering, it finally hit me, "Ya'know . . . it's probably just Japanese tourists . . . or some film company or sumpthin getting shots of the sign."

"Yeah . . . . . . as if the cops are gonna send helicopters up for 30,000 dollars a minute," and we both laughed at our ridiculous panic.

After another minute or so of hovering and

humming like a Hummingbird before our nectar, it finally flew off back towards the Griffith Observatory.

As soon as it was gone and we exhaled, Johnny realized, "Damn! We should've mooned it!"

And as we popped the last still-cold one and puffed a final tasty California cigarette, we reflected on where the hell we were. Not just the Hollywood Sign conquering — but we'd just inducted Jack & his Pops into the Counterculture Hall of Fame in Amsterdam 18 months ago, slayed it yesterday with S.A. in L.A., and now had the big Northport *Big Sur* 40th anniversary celebration reading performance party coming up in July [see *The Northport Report* a couple stories ahead in this book!] and John's 50th b'day was looming in September — and we vowed, "We gotta keep takin' this Furthur."

"I'm down," Johnny B. Jammed.

"We gotta do some Cassady Hassady shows — I mean, wait — did I just say 'Hassady'?!" and we laughed.

"I'll put a man on it," Cassady tossed his stock line.

B: "All we need is a van and a million bucks."

J: "I'll meecha in Toledo."

B: "'Appearing, One Night Only!'"

J: "'The Neal Cassady Tragedy Tour.'"

B: "'Sex, Drugs & Rock n Roll — The Formative Years.'"

J: "A 'prequel' as they say in this town."

B: *"How The Man Begat The Book That Begat The Legend."*

J: "Man, it's all too much. . . . . Too much happening. There's more books and biographies than I can ever read!

I can't keep up!"

B: "I know! It's growing crazy!" as we both thought of all the madness of the proliferation of the last few years.

"But this ain't!" John said as he held both his hands outstretched to the landscape before us — always a guy to see what is.

"Or this," and I waved mine up at the giant white letters towering above us, and we both beamed a victory nod.

Wherever we went, we went for it. Rode it. Pushed it. Took it a little bit Furthur than it's gone before. Made each other laugh or shared some tidbit with nearly every exchange. We were always having a good time — and always on *a Mission*. We rarely heard — or accepted — a "No" and, to the playful contrary, were always celebrating his Dad's "Yes Yes Yes!"

In America, when the sun beats down, and we stand at the base of the old broken-down Hollywood Sign watching the long, long skies over L.A. and sense all that raw Adventure still ahead of us, and all that Road going, all the people dreaming in the immensity of it, and in the Nickelodeon studio audience the children must be laughing in a world where they let the children laugh, and tonight the stars'll be out on the red carpet again, and don't you know that God is the Owsley Bear? The *Dark Star* must be soaring and shredding her sparkler dims over the amphitheaters of the prairies, which is just before the coming of complete night that blesses the earth, darkens the rivers, cups the Hollywood Hills and folds in the final Pacific shore, and nobody, nobody knows what's going to happen to anybody besides the forlorn rags of growing old. I think of John Cassady, I even think of Old Neal Cassady the father we never found. I think of John Allen Cassady.

3

The On The Road Scroll Auction

This was written contemporaneous with the event and is presented here unchanged from that day, including the original formatting. It was published in a couple places, and circulated widely via email in the early days of that medium. Jim Irsay and his team liked it so much they invited me to the Scroll's world premiere later that year and asked me to read at it.

Event: On The Road *scroll auction*
Date: May 22nd, 2001
Location: Christie's Auction House, 20 Rockefeller
    Plaza, Midtown Manhattan
Written: May 2001
Published in: Bob Holman's About Poetry website; The
    Kerouac Rag #3, Spring 2005

Part I — The Author's Song

The passing of the scroll . . .

It's gone to a good place . . .

. . . with an iconoclastic, white-tie-wearin' John Lennon lovin' "huge Bob Dylan fan," spirit of the '60s, buddy of Brinkley's, crony of Thompson's, and owner of the Indianapolis Colts (my new and forever favorite team), Jim Irsay.

It was football that got Jack out of Lowell,
and it was football that saved his holy scroll.

. . . it's late in the game — the secret weapon — a long bomb from Brinkley caught on the 2 million yard line by Irsay fresh off the bench, dodges past Sterling Lord on the 1 yard line — touchdown!

$2.2 million dollars — a new world record for an original manuscript, more than James Joyce's *Ulysses*, which some people think is a pretty good book, more than Kafka's *Trial* (the prior record holder) and every other literary manuscript ever sold. In fact, it comes to about $2,430,000 when you add in the commission and taxes.

I'd tell you about visiting the scroll
Four out of five days you could see it unrolled,

74

**But I'll save that for another time
Cuz the essence of the moment is the auctioneer's
rhyme ...**

The first time the scroll was ever unfurled and displayed in public.

I went over to Christie's at Rockefeller Center across
from NBC and next door to *The Today Show* at about
11:30AM to register so I wouldn't have trouble getting in
later. They asked me how much the bank could clear me
for. I wrote down some absurd amount, which actually
was my accumulated debt, now that I think of it, not
my plus column. So I was literally sweating it out in the
humid high noon heat till the Christie's cutie came out
and said, "I can't get anybody on the phone at Citibank.
They keep giving me the runaround. Here, just sign this
Credit Check form and here's your paddle." Whoopee
Cushion! I was in! Swingin' paddle #427.

Returning around 2:45, I walked again through the opulent and decidedly un-Beat Christie's Palace past the 6-foot wall mountings of animals in foliage like 3D Rousseaus, and climbed the ornate inner staircase two cushioned steps at a time until my bean crested the second floor and I immediately saw a mob filling the doorway and spilling into the hallway from the auction room (oh-oh!), the same as where the scroll had been displayed. I squeezed through like I had a seat, got to the front of the mob (something I seem to have a knack for) and lo — there it was — the packed in-action auction room! There were 120 seats (one for every foot of his scroll!), all filled, with about 25 people standing on each side, so maybe 175 in all, plus 12 Christie's suits manning rows of telephones on either side of the rectangular room, and about 20 people in the press corral at the back with five major camera set-ups, but none with network logos.

There were several assorted Sampases, Doug Brinkley, Sterling Lord, Ann & Sam Charters, Regina Weinreich, Michelle Esrick, Ed Adler, and scattered throughout was the hard core group of five of us who were there at closing time on the last visitation day: photographer Aaron Schumann and writer Ken Caffrey in the press pen, writer Ronna Johnson who's coming out with a second take on Women of The Beats later this year, and New York Beat guitarist Randy Hutton who we'll be hearing more from before long. Others too in the eternity of it.

And I'm there tryin' to figure it out — who's with who, what's goin' on. It's Lot number 242 when I came in. Jack's scroll soul is number 307. A guy gets up from a seat in the back row right in front of me. I hesitate maybe 10 seconds, then step forward before someone else reaches their courage threshold and I ask the next seated person if he's gone for good and get this rich suit's disdain, "I have no idea." Which I interpret as Snagged! Homie's home. Howdy doody and a whole lot more!

Part II — The Auctioneer's Song

There are rows of people and the flashing of paddles as the auctioneer speeds through oodles of numbers, pointing out bidders like a presto allegro conductor. But — sure looks like it's goin' to a telephone bidder, I think immediately, as they're lined up like stoic, somber six-gun shooters facing down each other across the room, concentrating, in their zones, conferrin' with the coach on the phone-gun, "When do I pull the trigger, chief?"

The bidding increments are all predetermined. Over $1,000, each next bid is $100 — so if you bid, that's your bid — you can't pick an amount. Over $5,000 it goes up $500 with each bid. Over $10,000 it goes up $1,000 every time. Over $1 million it goes up in $100,000 increments. When it hits $2 million it starts going up in $200,000 steps. But by then it's startin to get outta my range.

Up above the auctioneer is an electronic board that lists the lot number and current bid in U.S. dollars. Below that are lines with each country's equivalent monetary value — so as the auctioneer's zipping up the numerical ladder, all these foreign currency values are flapping by like the track-changing sign at Penn Station. Euros, UK pounds, French francs, Swiss francs, Deutsche marks, yen and lira in ooos, and the good old Canadian dollar squeakin' in on the bottom line. (We exist! In fact, in a general sense, there really was one of those "we exist" feelings in the room. It was the magic zing of the old Jack ring!)

So the auction's goin' by lickety-split. Lot 249, a copy of *Ulysses* signed by Joyce himself and by — get this — Matisse! (Who I always remember for saying, "Work cures everything.") "Okay, I'll open the bidding at 5 thousand ... 55 ... 6 thousand ..." and 20 seconds later, "Sold for $13,000 to paddle number 319 in the fourth row." And it all happens in less than a minute. The big ones take maybe a minute and a half, but lots of stuff's goin' for under 10 grand, all sorts of little things, no idea what they are, but I felt like bidding just 'cause they're so cheap. Hey — I'm cleared for it! It had to be something cool, right? Some Emerson thing. But there's the catch. You can't scratch your nose or anything. Like, if you move your arm you might be bidding. Then of course your nose would get itchy, and you'd have to turn away from the auctioneer like he's the teacher at school and sneak a scratch.

So you're watchin' your moves, watching the crowd, and watching these people watching their catalogues and marking in scores and bidding up to a certain point on lots, and then when their last item of the day is gone, they immediately get up and leave. Professional buyers. People with money. A set of Oxford dictionaries goes for $850,000! (And I bet it's used!) An autographed copy of *To Kill A Mockingbird* for $18,000. I keep wondering, "Who *are* these people?" The guy sittin' next to Doug Brinkley gets up and steps out for a minute at about lot 270. He's a big guy wearing this striped suit like I don't know what, a '20s gangster? A '40s hipster? I don't know. Big white tie on big black shirt, hair greased straight back, almost like a football player but with a cuff-linked Four Seasons polish and rock 'n' roll swagger.

By the time we get to lot 300 there are only four gunslingers left on the sideline phonelines as the auctioneer's still rattlin' through numbers like he's unloading on Bonnie & Clyde's car, ratta-tat-tatting by the thousands, 9 thousand, 10 thousand, my whole life savings and net worth flashing by in split seconds for some piece of autographed paper. Holy Zippers! "15 thousand... 24 thousand... 45 thousand, fair warning at 45 thousand... sold for 45 thousand." An Edith Wharton letter goes for only $800. Bargain. Musta been a crummy letter. "Went for a walk, love Edith." "Lot number 305 — Oscar Wilde, *The Importance of Being Earnest*, one of only 12 orange paper copies like it, inscribed by the author, opening with a tie bid at 15 thousand dollars, somebody want to break it? Thank you, 16 thousand dollars, 17 thousand..." etc. Goes to 60,000 in 60 seconds.

Part III — The Bidder's Song

Then comes the finale, "Lot number 307. The Lot *a lot of you* have been waiting for ...." (Ha-ha, a little auctioneer's humor.) "Jack Kerouac's original typescript scroll of *On The Road*, shown here before you on the screens. I'll start the bidding at 650,000 dollars on this ...." (I'm out.) "650,000 ... 700,000 ... 750,000 ... 800,000 ... 850,000 ... 900,000 ... 950,000 ... 1 million dollars over here, one million dollars in the front row, 1,100,000 dollars ... (pause) ... 1,200,000 ... 1,300,000 ... (pause) ... 1,400,000 (over the phone) then quickly 1,500,000 ... (pause)..." And all this time it's Brinkley's buddy who's flashin' up his white paddle #479 as soon as anyone else bids anything — the old Instant Paddle Flash Routine — then after a pause the front row finally bids again. "1,600,000 ... (then quickly) 1,700,000 ... (pause) 1,800,000 ... then Boom 1,900,000 ... (extended pause) ..." It's totally silent in the room, of course — you could hear a dream pop. "We can wait a little bit," the animated auctioneer allowed. "1,900,000 ... (long pause) ... The bid is 1,900,000 with the gentleman ... 1,900,000 ... Anybody say 2 million?" He looks down at the front row and says, "No, I'm sorry, 2 million's next ... 1,900,000 ... 1,900,000 then? In the third row at 1,900,000 ... (pause) Is there any further advance at 1,900,000? (pause) Fair warning at 1,900,000 ..." He raises his little wooden gavel stub and slowly begins to bring it down. "Last call ... " Then suddenly — "2 million!" he exclaims and points to the front row! Whoooa! Then instantly — "2,200,000." The whole crowd whoops — huge tension release — laughing, clapping, but all the way pinning-the-needle and then totally quiet again in about 2 seconds — flying by fast as bebop! "Anticipation!" says the auctioneer, articulating the air of the collective moment. "2,200,000 ... 2 million 2 ... (pause) At 2,200,000, in the third row. Are we all done at 2,200,000? (pause) SOLD! At 2,200,000!" And the whole room explodes in applause! Huge release — K'BAM!

And just as the applause is dying down, the auctioneer steps up again. "Ladies and gentlemen, I'd just like to announce that that is **a new world record for a literary manuscript at auction.**" And another round of cheering and whooping!

Then, in The Funny Beat Thing Dept., as soon as the final clapping dies down, some guy yells, "Corso lives!" and throws his fist in the air. This would not have worked in the middle of the auction, but it was funny as hell in the weird million-dollar-air-void afterwards to hear a prankster beat voice howling through the twinkling cosmos, "Corso lives!" He certainly does.

And 2 million dollars says, so does our man Jack.

It was all decided in under two minutes. And as soon as it was over, I bolted up front, and the first sign I had that everything was okay was Doctor Doug grinning so wide I thought his face would snap! Brinkley beamin' like a baby was all I needed to see. If he's happy, I'm happy. This must be a good thing!

I said a quick hi to Michelle Esrick and Casey Cyr, the only two other groovers who were at both the downtown *On The Road* show that I'd just produced at the Chelsea Commons on the 50th anniversary of the scroll's birthday and also at the uptown auction where it finally would get its wings and leave its New York home for the first time. Jack's tracing paper science project has outlived him. When I spoke to David Amram on the phone afterwards he was getting kind of choked-up about it — that Jack died with $83 in his pocket, and now just 30 years later, a notebook in that same pocket was worth more than he was.

And it turns out that the striped-suited football player who'd walked by earlier was the guy who bought it! He was all red-faced and excited and stunned — and he wasn't goin' anywhere. So I walked over and there was an AP reporter there asking him questions — but it's about . . . football ... ?! Huh? It's so weird to think there may be something bigger in this guy's life today than buying the *On the Road* scroll for two million bucks!

At least that's what the AP guy was opening with. He was talking divisional realignment with the retractable-dome blues again, and it was like — Weird Scene Channel Surf. Where's the remote? Switch back to the Jack Epiphany Channel, eh? Sudden click and Irsay's laughing, "Yeah, it's been a busy day." And while he's laughing a few other reporters surround us, then some big cameras, other people, boom mikes float in overhead . . . .

How does it *fe-e-e-el?*

Outside Christie's with the giant Scroll display in the window.

Part IV — The Acquiring Mind's Song

Jim Irsay: "Well, ya know, it's just ... it's exciting. Ya know, I look at it as a stewardship. I don't believe that you own anything in this world. It's dust to dust. It's something that I take as a responsibility, being a writer myself (!) knowing the sweat and the blood that went into creating something like this, and knowing how much people love the piece — that's all very important to me. Having the football team, how our fans love and cherish that. It's the same thing with something like this. It's great for Jack, right now, wherever his spiritual vibes are floating around, that he can be fulfilled, because as a writer, there's always this seed of doubt you have. You know, is it good enough? Is it worthy? Can it stand up with others? And a lot of times great artists end up dying before the world ever tells them what great artists they were. In his case, obviously this got published, but it left him a little bitter over some of the rejection, and so what a great honor for him that he and the manuscript can be celebrated today."

"What would he think of his work coming out of storage and selling for a record amount?"

"I'm sure he'd be just flabbergasted. It's exciting for me — that my grandparents got off the ships from Hungary and Poland right here at Ellis Island with nothing but the clothes on their backs — and you know, that's what this country's all about. And I think he would be amazed. These days, people — more so than 50 years ago — if you think you have some talent, you don't throw anything away. Like John Lennon, you know, I'm a big Lennon fan, and he used to curse his aunty, 'You'll regret throwing my drawings away. They'll be worth something someday.' So now of course everything is kept and treasured. I think there's a lot of great intrigue with this, tying in the Beat Generation and Cassady, Burroughs, Ginsberg, those guys had a huge influence on the cultural revolution in the sixties, and people like the Beatles and Bob Dylan, they had such a big influence, and to me that's really exciting — to be able to rub shoulders with the seed planters. The flowers are always beautiful, but the people who planted the seeds, the people who, in their time, had a way of looking at things differently, and had the courage to talk and to write and to live about it, that's what changes the world."

"Will you publish it?"

"A couple of things are planned. Sometime in the next coming months, somewhere in Indiana, I'll probably put it on display at a museum. We've talked to a couple of people about that. In 2007 I thought about having the 50th anniversary of the actual publication where maybe we'll do a tour. We'll follow the actual book's journey and have the scroll do the tour of the country and kind of mirror that journey. We have Dr. Douglas Brinkley here who is involved. He's the authorized biographer for Jack and he and I've discussed some various things. I actually tried to have **Hunter Thompson** in here today, I almost had him on the plane but then he turned back." (laughs.) "I thought that would liven up things a little bit." (louder laughter, then he looks directly at the cameras) "Hunter, if you're out there, we miss you." (and laughs again)

"Why did he turn back?"

"I don't know, it was a late night phone call and it just didn't happen. I think he wanted to watch the Laker game," he says laughing.

Then I asked him — "Will scholars other than Douglas be able to have access to studying the scroll?"

"Y'know, certainly. I'm very open-minded in terms of people who love it and want to have an opportunity to see it and be around it. That's what it's about. Like I said, I don't view it as something I own. Someone else will have it when I'm gone, and someone else will have it when they're gone. It's for the future generations. You love to see the kids and people who are influenced by the book have a chance to get up and be near it. To me, trying to let fans see it and people who have an interest in it, I'm very much open-minded to try to do that."

Then I asked a follow-up — "Would you expose the whole 120 feet when you did it in Indianapolis?"

"You know, that's what I think has to be talked about.
I really think one of the interesting things about this
manuscript is the unique way that it was written, and
the way that it's comported, it's the length minus the
bit that the dog bit off." (laughing) "It's too bad they
couldn't auction off the dog collar of the dog — that would
probably have brought in some good money here today."
(laughing)

"You'd have bought it, right?"

Laughing, "That would have been a good thing to
combine it with."

"What was the first Beat literature you ever read?"

"I would say, *Naked Lunch*, for me was, uh, and for me,
I'm a huge Bob Dylan fan. I've had the honor to be with
Bob several times and get to know him a little bit and
you know certainly his writing and singing brought me
to the doorstep of people like Jack, and people like Dylan
Thomas who had a piece sold here."

Then some guy asks him to sign a little rubber football,
joking that it'll be worth something in a few years. While
he's doing this the AP guy asks, "Jim, you said you were a
writer. What do you write?"

"Poetry and songs. I'm a guitarist as well. I actually
have an Elvis Presley guitar that he strummed — but for

anyone out there, if you have a John Lennon, I would trade the Elvis for the Lennon," he says (laughing again).

"You went awfully high on this; were you willing to spend more to buy this?"

"Yeah, it wasn't important to me, I just wanted to make sure we kept it in this country, kept it in America, you know, just have the ability for people to be able to share it and enjoy it. I'm just a fan like anyone else of it, and to me it's important to make sure it doesn't get locked away somewhere or get taken away to a far distant place or something like that."

"Did you walk in here expecting to spend a record amount for a manuscript?"

"Yeah. I was willing to spend a lot more!" he says, laughing loud, as does everyone else. "I won't tell you what my max was ...." (laughing) "I have to keep that a secret. Let me just say $10 million would not have frightened me away. I have a feeling — unless my fellow owner Paul Allen was goin' against me I think I woulda got it, but if Paul was here I must admit I would have been beaten," he says laughing.

"Do you want to read it off the scroll?"

"Yeah, that would be — but we have a dog at home who's very aggressive so we should keep that away from him," and everyone laughs.

"How old were you when it was published?"

"I'm 41, so I wasn't born. I was born in '59."

Then Rosebud Pettet perks up beside me and says —
"This gentleman here," and she points at me (!) "put
together *On The Road* marathon readings a few weeks
ago in LA and New York ..." (and I'm thinking, No way
— she's talking about *me!?!* This keeps getting weirder!)
"Are you planning, since you've got the scroll, to do any
celebrations on Jack in your hometown or wherever you
plan to keep it?"

"Sure, I'm open-minded to it. I think that Dr. Brinkley, as
well as my publicist Myra Borshoff, you know, will have
a say. I'm open to hear what people want to do with it.
Again, just to be able to share it and have fun with it and
celebrate it. Definitely that's what it's about, so I'm open-
minded to any of those sort of fun things."

Then the AP guy jumps in again, "Dr. Brinkley, I'd like to
know what you think, as a scholar, the significance of this
is now, the fact that this went for such big bucks, what
does this all mean?"

Brinkley: "That Jack Kerouac's become one of the writers
that people care about. That he's like Hemingway or
Fitzgerald or Faulkner, and even more so from a cultural

point of view. As Jim says, *On The Road* is a book that changed a lot of people's lives. It's a coming-of-age novel. And more than any other 20th century American literary document, there's a greater interest in the history and mythology of this particular manuscript than any other one that anybody can think of. It's unique, and it not only solidified the Beat Generation, but it also set into motion the notion of 'First thought — best thought,' spontaneity in literature, and then, as Jim said, it influenced so many people into the '60s. People like Thomas Pynchon who credits Kerouac's *On The Roa*d, to people like Bob Dylan, on down today to the music world, people like Lou Reed and Tom Waits. It's never-ending, Kerouac's influence. And for people that love *On The Road*, it's exciting that Jim has it, because he has this very open heart and wants to bring it first to the heartland for people to come see, and then have it tour the country eventually for the 50th anniversary of *On The Road*, so you couldn't be doing any better than that."

"What can you learn looking at the scroll that you can't from reading the book?"

Brinkley: "A lot. It's different than the book, all the names are in it, so you actually see Allen Ginsberg's name, or Neal Cassady, the real people, there are no pseudonyms. And for people who enjoy Jack Kerouac — because he's trying to get the words quickly out of him — you can see how his mind works. And I think, more than anything, what an extraordinary typist he was! He would just type and type. One of his great gifts as a writer was his quickness. When you're trying to get your first-thought, best-thought out, being that quick a typist, as evidenced in the scroll, with so few changes and so many beautiful paragraphs — we were looking while we were sitting down, Kerouac writing about Indiana, coming in on a bus to Indiana with the corn husks piled up, and then necking with the girl all the way to Indianapolis. There's hardly a city in America that doesn't somehow make a cameo in *On The Road*, and that Kerouac doesn't have something that's spiritually poetic and apropos to say about it."

Irsay: "Plus the paddle, Doug. The paddle was 479, Jack's age, and 9, the year he died, '69, so it's 4-7-9, and Doug said that was a good omen right away."

AP: "Jim, are you kind of an All-American boy?"

"I'm not sure what that means."

Pause, stumble mumble bumble, "You're so American, it's unbelievable."

"I guess I am then, you know?" (laughing) "It's like George Harrison says, 'I hope they don't get time to hang a sign on me.' It's just a — a good thing to be called because I love this country."

And then your friendly Beat Reporter chirps in yet again!

Brian: "Do either of you think there's any preservation needed in the short term for it?"

Irsay: "That's something that I've consulted some experts on, and that's really important, to make sure that this thing can remain intact for a lot of years and be shown for many centuries."

Since that wasn't enough for me, I once again pushed the Follow-Up Button: "Was it the experts' opinion that anything needed to be done? Is it in okay shape?"

"Just that it's in real good shape considering the years. You know, the proper room temperatures and that sort of thing have to be looked at. When you start getting out there, 500 years, a thousand years, I think, you know, there's some erosion, it's inevitable, but we're gonna find ways to protect it, obviously."

Some new reporter announces himself and asks, "Jim, what does this purchase mean to you?"

"You know, it means a lot to really acknowledge people that stand and fight for the truth and what they believe in in their art, that ultimately it's rewarded and celebrated. And again, there's so many artists out there at this very moment who are working and some of them will die without ever really receiving any due for what they've done. But I think, anyone's human spirit, since you go back to the days of the cavemen, it's just expression, it's self-expression. People want to be recognized for having a feeling and sharing that with someone else, and I think that's what this acknowledges. And for me, it's just a lot of fun. I feel blessed to able to be here, and have gotten the manuscript, and just look forward to having a lot of fun with it, and sharing it, and celebrating it, because it's enjoyable. There's so many difficult things that go on in the world, it's nice to celebrate life. In the NFL we do that — entertaining people. I look at this the same way as being able to do that. My next goal is to be able to sit the scroll next to the Lombardi Trophy, you know? That's what you get for winning the Super Bowl, and we're real close, you know, and to have those two things together hopefully maybe by the end of January would be great," he says, laughing.

"Did you buy it individually, or did anybody go in with you?"

"No, just individually."

"How old were you when you read *On The Road*?"

"I read it about '77, and what it meant to me just being a teenager in the '70s, you know, freedom, rebellion, the things that a young person looks at in life, which is just — the journey — the excitement of the journey, the search for truth and meaning and the thrills of life. It's like Bob Seger said, 'I wish I didn't know now what I didn't know then,'" and he laughs again. "You gotta study that line hard to get the true meaning of that," and he laughs even harder. Then he says, "Well guys, thank you very much." And I say right to him and very soberly, "Thank you!" and we make serious direct eye contact. Something great had just happened.

There's a lot more that went on. What's above is the complete post-purchase impromptu news conference, minus the opening NFL realignment stuff, and a bunch of um's and you-know's. Afterwards, I surfed around and talked to John Sampas and asked if they were going to publish the text of the scroll, and he answered, I believe the exact word was, "Absolutely," but for sure I remember his expression, which was like — Duh, dumb question, *what do you think?*

Jim & the *New York Times* reporter over my shoulder.

Here's some random snippets caught from Irsay's sit-down interview with the *New York Times*:

"I'm a very big Dylan Thomas fan."

"When I saw this piece come available it really did grab my attention and I really wanted to seek it out and find out where this piece stood in the 20th century, in the context of the pieces that are out there, what others felt about it. There are people like Doug Brinkley who professionally deal in this, he's a writer himself, and just consulting a lot of friends, it feels like it appeals to a lot of different people."

"I'm originally from Chicago. My influences came a lot from rock music, particularly Bob Dylan and the Beatles, and you start going behind the situation and finding out who influenced them. Paul McCartney's worked with Ginsberg. Dylan, obviously, taking his name from Dylan Thomas, and coming to New York City in 1961, and his experiences, and through that, that's where the interest really came. I think people are influenced by the Beat Generation, and by Dylan, in ways that they don't even know. They may not even know of the individual, but society's been changed so much by them."

"Thanks a lot. I was a broadcast journalism major, so I'm a big fan of the *New York Times*."

"We're going to take good care of it, and we're going to

make sure the fans enjoy it — that's the main thing."

Okay, this is Brian, signing off from basecamp at Mount Kerouac. Back to you.

You and a guest
are cordially invited to the
Indiana debut of the

Original manuscript (scroll) of
On the Road by Jack Kerouac

Evening's Program

Welcome by Jim Irsay

Remarks by Mayor Bart Peterson

Music and Readings
featuring Patti Smith

Friday, September 14, 2001
Colts' Pavilion
Union Federal Football Center
7001 W. 56th St. Indianapolis
8:30 - 11 p.m.

Coffees and espresso
Desserts

Casual/Coffeehouse attire

No admission charged;
contributions of $25 per person
to Writers' Center of Indiana
are kindly requested

RSVP no later than September 7

Invitations are non-transferable and must be presented at the door

After I wrote the piece you just read and sent it to Jim Irsay's office, they invited me to the debut of The Scroll to the world. They also asked me to read something of my choice from the book along with Patti Smith, and to stay and enjoy the season opening Indianapolis Colts home game in the owner's box. But it all got canceled due to the tragic events of 9/11.

4

The Northport Report

This is another story written contemporaneously — in fact I started it within about two minutes of Johnny leaving my apartment in Manhattan. I was of a mind back then to capture the Beat events as they happened, and in fact had developed a practice (which I still maintain) of writing them (or at least starting them) even before going to sleep on the day the event happened — to capture the raw honest energy of the actual moment.

Event: Big Sur 40th anniversary marathon reading
Date: Sunday, July 22nd, 2001
Location: Northport, Long Island, New York
Written: July 2001
Published in: Beat Scene No. 39

Whale, we had another Jackfest — dancing with *Big Sur* by the Big Sea — this time in Jack's wave-lapping hometown of Northport, the idyllic little living Rockwell harbortown where he went to dock near the darkness of the city but still remain a slip away.

I'm just back from the novel-performing road trip with Cassady, and his bottle's still spinning on the table but not falling over as he's dashed out the door to JFK to hop the bird back to Cali, so before the body gets cold and the news gets old lemme be so bold as to share some gold . . . .

Sunday, July 22nd, 2001 began with a proclamation where the mayor gave Carolyn & John Cassady the keys to the city or some such thing at a very official ceremony. And as part of it, Carolyn read two revealing letters Jack wrote to her. One was from October '61, just after he finished writing *Big Sur*, and describes the big door bursting Cassady-Kerouac reunion scene in Ferling's tiny cabin that, wildly, we were all going to read together in a few hours. Both letters were full of longing and heart-felt passion — and as she's reading them Carolyn's just a beaming gem in a tender-heart treasure-chest. Jack and her were really close, and it's so beatifically beautiful that she was around for the whole weekend being open and accessible to anyone who wanted to talk.

Jack's beach under the Bixby Creek Bridge in Big Sur, circa 2001.

It was Sunday morning in the Universe, and this being the crumbling Empire of New York, there were no liquor stores open! So, Big Tim Moran and I — he was Edie, Henri & Huncke's friend — bolt back to our Chalet hideaway to collect the only bottle of cold white wine in town. It was a dizzy hounds of hair morning for more than just myself after a night of howling at the Jackmoon out on George Wallace's back deck. We were bad. Clearly needed some adult supervision.

Tim and I followed the directions to where the all-day reading of the novel would be, and he looked back at the notepaper and says, "That's it right there," pointing to a sign that reads "Northport Police Station"!

He kept driving looking for a parking spot as I was looking back over my shoulder, still seeing the word "Police," trying to shake the picture clearer in my beer-soaked lab, but it still — "Looks like that said 'Police Station' back there."

"Yeah," Tim burst out with a long-suppressed laugh. "That's where it is."

"Hmm," I say, turning around, trying to count how many laws I was breaking at the moment. "First time we ever played a cop shop," I Jaked to his Elwood.

We walked up the stairs and on the right was the door directly into the precinct, and in the center were two glass doors leading to . . . the county courtroom! Sure enough, we were celebrating Jack's judgement day novel in a court of law! There's a poem in there somewhere. But we must have been acquitted cuz in the end (tho I don't wanna give it away) we were all let go on our own recognizance.

Levi Asher and others were sitting up in the judge's bench area, there was a big camera from the Metro Channel in the witness stand, and the room was packed with rows of chairs that were all full in early excitement — a hundred people or more, then a spilling overflow anti-chamber room just outside the courtroom by the glass doors where the pacers and racers had a space to zoom. Printed on the front of the table with the participants' books and CDs for sale it said in big bold letters: "Defendants Stand Here" — as if we needed a reminder when we're admitting our guilty pleasure!

Outside the main doors, the front steps became the green room hang scene. You could just open the glass doors and hear the show from there, and sorta pick whichever chapter or reader you wanted to catch, then take a break and hang with the cigarette smokers and surreal surfers.

It became obvious that we needed a proper dressing room, so I brought out a nice chair for Saint

Carolyn By The Sea, and that pretty much evened out the Universe — except that we didn't have a corkscrew! We thought of going in the police station to see if they'd confiscated one recently, but instead I minded the boss and the store while John & Big Tim went across the street to the old brick house that was the Northport Hysterical Society with two old ladies behind glass-top counters containing artifacts and tiny labels like, "Hammer – circa 1850" or "Mabel – circa 1925."

"Um, do you have a corkscrew by any chance?" asks our dangerous duo. "No, I should say not!" Then Ambassador John turns on the charm and they get to talkin' and he says, "It's for me mum, she's the co-chair at your event across the street."

"Oh, who's she?" asks the inquisitive matron. John looks down at the countertop and there's a picture of her & Jack & John's two sisters. "That's her right there." And the motherly one behind the counter smiles and says, "Just a minute," and goes and unlocks one of the glass cabinets and takes out this large bone handle corkscrew that Walt Whitman used or something and goes, "Here, maybe this'll work."

So we popped open the bottle, and oh yeah, we'd brought one crystal goblet from the sweet suite, and got Carolyn perched on a throne sitting at the top of this grand staircase like Abe Lincoln, holding a glass of wine and holding court, surrounded by her coterie of boys as different people would come by to visit her. Most would squat down to be close, and each would have some story they wanted to share, always including the line, "I first read *On The Road* when I was X years old, and it changed my life . . . ." Eventually I snuck out a few more chairs and smuggled over some Heinekens from my secret iced 2-4 stash in the trunk and it evolved into a full-blown, feet-up, room-with-a-view backstage party — on the front steps of the Main Street police station at high noon on a Sunday!

Inside at the reading, David Amram was set up in the corner with his 7,000 instruments strewn all over the place, and drummer Kevin Twigg workin the brushes on a full kit, and bearded John Dewitt thrummin' the upright bass. There's about five different digi cameras rollin', and it looked like a two-camera shoot from The Metro Channel. There's musician-poet Casey Cyr, painter-poet Susan Bennett, installation artist China Blue, filmmakers and actors Michelle Esrick and Peter Gerety, architect and photographer Larry Smith, poet George Dickerson, and on and on.

And if this wasn't already enough of a Surreal Circus — in between some readers there were these . . . belly dancers! Ya'huh. Jingling little-bell-tingling colorfully costumed barefoot belly dancers weaving to Amram's best Middle-Eastern snake-charmer, and yer goin', "Okay, which one'a you Pranksters slipped the acid in my joe?"

Within this belly dancing 3-ring courtroom, some readers really rose to the occasion — including Levi Asher on chapter 9 who was understated and funny and riveting reading Jack's first sea-me breakdown. And then this actor John Ventimiglia who's in *The Sopranos* among other things, plays Artie the restaurant owner, he's way into Jack (had just played him in Joyce Johnson's play *Door Wide Open*) and as Johnny C. smiled later, "He sounded more like Jack than Jack does." He read chapters 10 and 11 including that great description of Lew Welch & Phil Whalen's S.F. Zen-East House crashpad.

And then this local woman Kate Kelly came up for chapter 12 and kicked the thing into another gear, being really passionate and playful and strong and forceful and funny, all done with a smile as Jack raged thru his confusion. Then, with Amram on piano, John Cassady read chapter 13 — and Johnny's funny cuz he throws in all these little asides and commentary on the text as it's passing. "'... in the old photo ...' Hey who took that? '... throwing tires all over the place ...' Oh this is so accurate, it's great," he says, laughing along to the quick memory movie. He picked chapter 13 cuz it's about their life in Los Gatos, and he's tossing off comments to his mom who's keeping a running commentary right back at him in a smile-sharing across a half-a-stage and half-a-century of them playing together.

After John read, we had a break until the three of us were on for our chapter 23 group jam, so we drifted down Main Street and popped into Gunther's Tap Room, Jack's old drinking hole, and you could see why — nuthin but a bar and a pool table. Except today there were just tons of people sitting around with orange & black *Big Sur* paperbacks in front of them. So we shambled off like dingledodies down the sidewalk like we've been doing all our lives until we found a front window booth in some joint who's motto was apparently: "If you want service, serve yourself." No sooner did we sit down than Levi and his sister Sharon came along (who was into the Beats before Levi was, we learned this weekend) and they stand there staring at the outside menu as we'd done seconds earlier and made the same call we did. And then Regina Weinreich ... and now there's a whole whack of us Beats munchin' the Big Cereal recovery brunchfast. But this is also how ya miss part of the show, you understand.

So of course I get us back to the gig about 5 minutes before we're supposed to go on, as Carolyn proclaims with a raised I-told-you-so finger, "Brian gets things *done!*" followed by a big smile and laugh. She's been riffing that refrain since we first started hanging together and by now it's become a running joke.

For my reading, even before we knew they were coming to Northport, I'd picked chapter 23 about the Cassadys arriving at the cabin and surprising Jack and McClure. I wanted to do it justice if they weren't gonna be here to do it themselves (it is a courtroom after all) — then Lo and Behold! The Angels! They showed! So we weaved it into having John do the Neal & "Timmy" parts, Carolyn doing her parts, and me playing narrator Jack. We'd read together in Amsterdam — the first time John & Carolyn ever performed together thanks to *High Times* and the Cannabis Cup of all things — then John and I just did a duet in L.A. at the Jack scroll-writing celebration that S.A. Griffin & I put together for the Jack-finishing-*On The Road*-Day April 22nd, so we were already old hams at this.

John & Carolyn — first time ever on stage together —
Amsterdam, Monday, Nov. 22nd, 1999.

And it was funny cuz everybody else was reading solo and suddenly we're a trio with god knows what kind of crazy improv winginess, and I'm sure ol' producer George Wallace was kinda, "Oh jeez, what are these guys gonna *do*?!" 'Course, we had no idea either. We'd gotten together the afternoon before and attempted to block out paragraphs and passages, but we were all just seeing each other for the first time in ages and were much more gushy gooey gabby than any kinda rehearsey.

And it was funny — I was tryin to funnel some passages to Carolyn cuz she didn't have too many "lines," and each time I'd pass something over she'd scan down it and go, "Aaaaa no." She loves the writing but it's too close to home and there's some pretty graphic details about ol' Cody's lovelife. But it also has the stuff about Carolyn having two husbands for a while, which she loves, so we just went, "Ah, wheel wing it. No potholes on this golden road."

When we started, Amram was just taking off for his soundcheck at his evening concert, but our "song" was gonna be so chaotically theatric we'd be more than making our own music! We were bouncing back & forth like Abbott & Costello, with John taking the McClure dialogue so we got to perform the cabin rap in two voices, and then he also rode the "Boom!" Cassady-bursting-in-the-door scene. When Jack lists the kids' character names, John started laughing at his sister Jami's Jackname 'Gaby.' "See, that's so perfect for her cuz she used to get up on his knee and just gab-gab-gab-gab-gab," he laughed out loud.

Ferlinghetti's tiny but legendary Big Sur cabin, circa 2001.

And John took off on the Neal raps, channeling his Pop, rollin' fast like the road, with animated hand gestures, laughin', goofin', playin'. When Cody's trying to think of his new jeep's color, Carolyn yells out "Grape!" At Jack's comical adage for Neal — "He Lived, He Sweated" — John cracks up and starts doing this classic Cassady Sweating Shuffle dance at the podium, laughin' and hemmin' 'n' hawin' and ah-shucksin' and ya-had-to-be-therein', then laughs again and says, "Ah man, that's the best line in the book. I'm only serious."

At Carolyn's dialogue we all got it about half right, which of course made it even funnier, and everybody's laughin' but it's workin', and there's Carolyn gentle and petit and lady-like laughing away and gamely trying to hit her mark, and it was a sweet tender family-beaming moment in Beatport.

After the reading we all went off on a wild adventure to two of Jack's three houses in town. The first at 34 Gilbert was *Really Nice!* Couldn't believe it. He bought it for $14,000 in March '58 on a one-afternoon road trip with Robert Frank and Joyce Glassman (Johnson) just after *On The Road* splashed down. It's a large Victorian, 50 years old when he bought it, with brown shingle siding, a big front porch, high front hedge, massive tree in the backyard, and a big old double garage for both the cars he couldn't drive. The house has three floors, with an attic garret for his writing zone, and as Levi kept commenting on, this beautiful stained-glass window in the front, looked like a reclining cubist nude, maybe 3′ wide, 18″ high. "You'd think this would have made it into the fiction somewhere," Levi says.

So we take a buncha snaps with Levi and John and China Blue and Anthony who booked us in Amsterdam and who grew up right behind Jack's house here as he tells us about Mémère inviting them in for cocoa in the winter and disheveled Jack shuffling around in his terrycloth bathrobe and bedroom slippers.

All weekend there were different people with different memories of Jack. The artist Stanley Twardowicz was softly sharing stories of their drinking exploits, and Larry Smith who took their pictures remembering the mix of solemness and revelry, and all these other locals with little anecdotes about him. He really did live in Northport a long time — April '58 to September '64, minus a few brief excursions to Orlando.

Stanley was a great guy, by the way. Very friendly and open and sensitively remembering his old friend. Larry Smith had a few photos he'd never had published that were haunting. One of them from '64 gave Carolyn the willies. "It's all in there. It's all in those eyes," she'd say emphatically pointing and shivering all over.

We also went to his second house at 49 Earl Avenue after comically getting lost for about 500 hours. This was the "secret hideaway" he moved to after he sold Gilbert Street and their plans to build a house in Florida fell through — and where he was living when he took the Big Sur trip. He bought it in part for the finished basement he envisioned as his study, but later insulated the attic and put in a little electric fireplace to warm his crow's-nest. It looks smaller than Gilbert, and did indeed have "the six-foot fence I'd built around my yard for privacy," as he describes in *Big Sur* — a high old stockade style that you couldn't see thru or get over. In fact Jack climaxes *Big Sur* right here on Earl with, "The corner of the yard where Tyke is buried will be a new fragrant shrine making my home even more homelike somehow — On soft Spring nights I'll stand in the yard under the stars — Something good will come out of all things yet —" And sitting on the front step of the house watching us watch the house was this big warm friendly calico cat, who never laid down or ran scaredy-cat away, but rather held there, saying, "Hello. Yes. I'm here."

We never did find 7 Judyann Court, but wheel be back cuz we were all fully stoked about this fairy-tale of a town with its salty harbor and sultry air. I mean gorgeous — quaint old-world Main Street with windy tree-covered sideroads, surrounded by hills 'n' sails, and nooks 'n' grannies. "Why didn't Jack write more about *this* place?" Carolyn kept asking. The beauty of the town was really the surprise hit of the weekend for all of us. We were fully bummed we didn't catch more of the readers, but it was such a gorgeous day and there were seven or eight Adventure Cards on deck. Had t'play 'em.

After the tour, we all went out for this enormous steak dinner following a tip from a local actor Cassady'd dubbed John Goodman — and we took over the place. It was your jumbo grill here's-the-beef kinda joint where we could only get a big table in the non-smoking section, so we'd keep leaving our spread completely empty like a Dine 'n' Dash and huddle in the smoking corner while our sad plates sat there silently steaming.

We eventually headed to Amram's show late as hell, got lost s'more, and when we finally found the park in the dark there was this flood of people leaving with lawn chairs and blankets, and we were like, "Whoops!!" Carolyn and John were supposed to read some Jack with Dave's band. So we wagged up with our tails between our legs — but thank gawd he was just takin' a break and there was a whole second set!

I spotted Jason Eisenberg, the wild Lord Buckley channel who read chapter 18 and was probably great but we missed him when we went for that surreal recovery brunch, so he & I snuck away for a colorful confab & jazz cigarette in the holy gazebo in the back of the park and riffed on the Universe as Dave wailed away on Ellington and Monk down the dark treed hill below us.

Then Carolyn came out to the microphone and read the part of *On The Road* where Jack's "on the rooftop of America," at The Great Divide, yelling across the plains to an old man with white hair walking toward him with "the Word." Then John came out and knocked it out of the Harry Chapin Park — probably his best reading ever. Like a blues player he sang, "I'll be seeing old Denver at last." By this time I'd weaved back down to sit on the blanket spread with Levi and his parents & sister right at the foot of the stage, and while John was riffing, Levi leaned in and whispered, "He's channeling Neal."

Then local hero George Wallace closed the show with the classic last paragraph of *On The Road*, which was just singled out and praised by the *New York Times'* Editorial Page earlier this year. He read with this quiet sadness that almost made me cry, and it sounded like he was going to break down himself and could barely choke out the words, "I think of Dean Moriarty."

So, there it is. I believe there may have been some drinking involved. Some folks are real straight and some folks are nine-bottles-later. It was pretty funny. But everyone was golden and glistening. It was really ... small town niceness. The locals are living near enough to New York City that there's still a healthy voltage surging through them, and they're passionate about words & self-expression and being yourself — all while living in a Norman Rockwell painting — just really good people ... with a penchant for partying in police stations.

5

On The Road
to
The Hall of Fame

This was the first story written for this book. In fact, it was originally written as the beginning of the book. Eventually as the other pieces came into play it made more sense to structure them chronologically — but this is how I thought this book was going to open. The story is constructed from handwritten notes, 12 pages of contemporaneous typed notes, roughly 30 digi audio recordings, and hundreds of photos.

Events: On The Road premieres; and Cassady & Hassett at the Grateful Dead at the Rock n Roll Hall of Fame
Date: November 2012
Locations: Bloomington, Indiana; Columbus, Ohio; Rock n Roll Hall of Fame, Cleveland, Ohio; The Roads in between
Written: April 2018

I first saw Cassady again not long after my mother died.

We had just gotten over a serious election that I won't bother to talk about, except that it had something to do with car elevators in home garages, and my feeling that I had to go see The Dead. With the coming of that band and that dude began the part of my life you could call my life seeing *On The Road*.

I was about to catch my third movie premiere in as many countries. In the last couple months, I'd been at the first screening in the U.K., at the palatial Somerset House along the Thames in downtown London, then the World Premiere of the final cut at the Toronto International Film Festival — and now it was screening for the first time in the Midwestern lands where this prairie boy was raised — before its big premieres in New York & L.A. next month.

Bloomington, Indiana — November 2012 — Obama had just won a second term, the world was not yet coming to an end, and Indiana's own Republican Richard Mourdock had contributed quite helpfully by saying during a debate that abortions should be illegal even in the cases of rape, apparently unaware there were cameras rolling

Now here I was driving from Camp Canada to Camp Kerouac, going On The Road to the home of The Scroll and its curator Jim Canary to meet up with its film director Walter Salles and the son of its hero John Allen Cassady to see what happens. Then we'd be driving from red Indiana to blue Ohio for the Grateful Dead's massive special exhibit at the Rock n Roll Hall of Fame in Cleveland — the ever connection of Jack & Jerry, the soundtrack to *The Road, Goin' Down It Feelin' Good*, with Grateful Dean and the big eyes beamin' while silver screens flicker and pranksters jigger the lights and the sound that's all around and tell the stories that are still untold while the Road unfolds.

Bloomington would soon become my second home due to a certain Wizard of Wonder (see the *And Other Adventure Tales* part of *How The Beats Begat The Pranksters)* but this was the first time Cassady or I would ever set foot in the place.

John was named by his parents Neal & Carolyn for their closest friends Jack (John) Kerouac and Allen Ginsberg. He's the only person on Earth named for three of the four faces on the Mount Rushmore of Beatlandia. Neal said he didn't name him "Jack" because, "No son of mine is going to go through life being called a Jack-assady," but he still got the sound in there with the initials — J.A.C.

John and I first met in New York in the '90s over a show I produced at The Bitter End on Bleecker Street in Greenwich Village celebrating Levi Asher's LitKicks'

(Literary Kicks) 5-year anniversary of being the first site dedicated to the Beats on the internet. John and I had been corresponding for years — but that was the first time we were in the same place at the same time.

The Literary Kicks Summer Poetry Happening
July 21st, 1999

We already shared a love of Adventure, a goofy sense of humor, and an appreciation for adult beverages. The moment it first kicked in just who I was becoming friends with was at the Chelsea Hotel, where Levi, God bless 'im, had put up John for this LitKicks anniversary. We were all having a big party in his room, as is our wont, with everybody off yakking away, and John and I were sitting with our backs to the wall on either side of a little round hotel room table, watching and listening to the chaos of collected crazies as we laughed along and tossed in one-liners when they hit us.

At some point at that little table, I said for the first time, "Cassady, pass me the lighter."

"Huh," thought I. "I just asked Neal Cassady to pass me a lighter." Okay, not the real deal Neal, but the real Cassady. This wasn't a Cass*idy*, or just any puffing Chelsea denizen that I was sitting in the middle of 10 floors of — this was "Neal's kid," as Jerry Garcia and the other members of the Dead called John since the first time his Dad introduced them in the mid-'60s.

And we weren't emailing — we were talking. There were a dozen or more SuperCool people in the room, but right from the git he & I paired off, and would blurt out comic asides, verbalizing some internal funny thought, not really concerned if anyone heard it or not, but John & I had tuned in each other's channel and always heard the other's lines.

He has a sense of humor and style of delivery exactly like another Kerouac friend Henri Cru who I also knew — dry, rich with stock phrases, and you have to know the person was joking or it might just sound like some illogical aside. But if *you knew* he was joking (which was all the time) both these two guys were funny as hell.

John and I would sit there at that little round table tossing off one-liners inspired by the room's calamitous clowning that for the most part nobody else heard, except us two wisecrackers sitting off stage.

It was at that little round Chelsea table that I first glimpsed what was going to become a lifelong friendship and Road partnership that would take us to Amsterdam and Greenwich Village and Northport and Los Angeles and Santa Cruz and San Francisco and gawd-nose where-all — but here we were now in Bloomington, Indiana.

This whole Adventure actually began in Toronto. See, also, "Making Better Time On The Road" in *How The Beats Begat The Pranksters*. Geez that book keeps coming up a lot!

Y'see, when *On The Road* first got made into a Major Motion Picture after a gazillion years of *not*, I was really struck by the Brazilian director Walter Salles. I'd watched the hour-long press conference from Cannes a few times, and really dug his sensibilities — how his mind worked, and the poetic way he spoke. I'm a big fan of the cinematic arts and study the heck out of it, and really wanted to get five minutes with this director — he just seemed like *such* an interesting guy.

That whole story's in that other book, but the short and the long of it is — with my Canadian Prankster brother Damo, we snuck backstage after the World Premiere of the final cut of *On The Road* at the Toronto International Film Festival and met Walter — you gotta read the whole story in that other book, it's freakin' amazing — but anyway he and I hit it off like lifelong friends right from the get-go. In fact, by the time we were at the New York premiere a couple months later, he was introducing me as his childhood friend.

He told me after the Toronto screening in September that he was going to be coming back for a series of screenings in the fall and asked if I'd like to join him. I'm a political animal and participatory activist, and even with my love for Kerouac and *On The Road* and all that, keeping a Democrat in the White House was the order of the day that 2012 fall.

When walter told me his screening tour dates in hopes I could join him somewhere, I saw that Bloomington was the week after the election — and knew that was also home to Jim Canary, the colorful manuscript preservationist who had been caring for the original *On The Road* scroll since it was bought by Indiana's own Jim Irsay back in 2001 — (see the *On The Road Scroll Auction* earlier in this book).

I'd always wanted to meet Jim Canary — he seemed so interesting and weird and one-of-us from everything I'd seen and heard about him — so Walter and I sort of zeroed in on the Bloomington screening, and as it was getting closer he emailed, "Wanna meet me in Indy?"

Then, as the Laws of Fate would have it — ol' Johnny and I were talkin' on the phone. One of the many things Walter & I had in common was a real love for both Carolyn and John Cassady. There was something about their warmth and intelligence, their smiles and twinkles. They were both firecracker smart, and easy to laugh, and generous with their time and spirit, and just fun to be around. Walter and I had talked about both John and Carolyn a bunch in person in Toronto and over email exchanges after that. So, when I was talking to J.C. I told him I was about to head to Bloomington to meet up with Walter.

Now, ol' Johnny, he hadn't been getting out too much. A few years earlier he'd teamed up with Jerry

Cimino who would soon found The Beat Museum in
San Francisco, and the two of them travelled around
the country in what they coined "the Beatmobile" — an
Airstream RV & trailer with all manner of Beat stuff in it,
and would do appearances all over talking about Cassady
and Kerouac and everything Beat. But since then, John
was kind of *Off The Road* as it were (and to name-check
his mother's great book). He and I had had so much fun
together in all those aforementioned cities, I just blurted
out, "Hey, you should come join us! I know Walter would
love to see you."

See … Johnny didn't really know that, or have it
fully internalized. As gregarious and outgoing as he can
be, he's also got a shy side. Maybe that's why we were
sitting against the wall at the Chelsea and not in the
middle of things. He didn't really know how positively
Walter spoke of him. But I did. That's why I had no
qualms about inviting him to join us. "Walter would love
to see you," I told him about five times, as the idea first
hatched and then formed over the course of the call.

And Bob Weird's your uncle and wouldn't
you know it, but ol' Johnny hopped on a plane to
Bloomingsville, as we took to calling it, and suddenly the
gang was united On The Road Again.

= * = * = * = * = * = * = * = * =

There we were on the campus of Indiana University, where the film department was hosting a week-long tribute to the director, including the Midwestern premiere of *On The Road*.

Indiana University is a goddamn gorgeous place. Founded when the state was, 1820, it's all post-modern castles built in a lyrical forest, with trails and paths and roads full of students texting and ear-phoning and go-karting around fountains, and with one of the most renown manuscript libraries in the world including everything from Shakespeare's first folio to a Declaration of Independence, but also all of Orson Wells' papers and an enormous music and film archive — the perfect place for an independent like Jack and his film to have their Midwestern bread-basket premiere.

Right outside this lazy hazy home and fancy new theater was a giant life-size bronze of Bloomington's native jazzman Hoagy Carmichael sitting at a Steinway writing a song, his jacket tossed over the lid and sheet music under one hand with the other on the keys as though he just ran home with a new melody he had to get down.

And in what I knew instantly was a Walter Salles touch — parked right next to the piano was a gorgeous 1949 Hudson, the exact make & model Neal Cassady bought and drove Jack & his friends in *On The Road*. "Oh man!" Johnny said as soon as we saw it. "Garrett [Hedlund] and I drove the one Walter used in the movie up from L.A. when he donated it to the Beat Museum. Whadda guy! It was a blast. We stopped and picked up Al [Hinkle] on the way. What a trip *that* was!"

"Oh geez! Cassady and Al Hinkle in a '49 Hudson! How did I miss that trip?!"

"Yeah — you shoulda been there," he laughed. "Walter called, and the next thing I knew I was in L.A.! And did they ever have that thing tricked out! There was a whole new motor in it — _man_ that thing could _fly!_" he laughed. "And they had these hidden compartments so you couldn't see all the new gages n shit — it was like

James Bond's car with all these secret gadgets."

"Oh yeah, speaking of James Bond," I said. "Jim Canary told me all of Ian Fleming's archives are here at the Lilly Library along with Jack's Scroll."

"Really?!" he laughed. "What _don't_ they have here?!" he said as we passed through the doors into the theater.

The '49 Hudson On The Road at *On The Road* in Indiana.

Walking down the aisle of the plush red velvet Thomas Hart Benton-muraled Indiana University Theater, Walter was already on stage introducing his *Searching For On The Road* documentary — one of only three times it would ever be screened in a theater — in San Francisco, Bloomington and New York City — and I was the only person in the world who was at two or more of them other than the director himself!

I saw his face light up as soon as he spotted his two

Road buddies rolling into the theater of the absurd.

This *Searching For OTR* turned out to be a great documentary — the medium Walter first began in as a filmmaker — and includes all sorts of new interviews with Gary Snyder, Al Hinkle, Carolyn at her house in England, Ferlinghetti, McClure, Diane di Prima, Hettie Jones, Joyce Johnson, Johnny Depp, Gore Vidal, David Byrne, Wim Wenders, Doug Brinkley, Peter Coyote, Bob Weir, and loads of others, plus cool video clips, like Coppola's original screen tests of Brendan Fraser for Sal, Matthew McConaughey for Dean, Jennifer Love Hewitt for Marylou, Russell Crowe for Old Bull Lee, and a great Ashley Judd doing Galatea, plus all sorts of details like how Jack tried to talk D.A. Pennebaker into making an *On The Road* movie (!) and how Jean-Luc Godard was once in the mix to do it in the early '80s with Dennis Hopper as a possible Dean, and talk of another version with famed Kerouac aficionado Johnny Depp for Sal and Sean Penn as Dean, who's in the doc pleading for good actors to be cast now that he is over-aged for the role.

A funny classic moment happened when Al Hinkle was on screen telling a story about he and Neal, and he mentioned, "There may have been a little bit of marijuana involved," and both John & I spontaneously blurted out-loud in unrehearsed harmony — "A *little* bit?!"

After the screening, Walter had to go and do press or something, so freshly-arrived Johnny and I had some time to catch up and prankster about. Just as we were plotting which direction to go chase college girls, this serious guy comes up with a couple thousand dollars worth of cameras hanging around his neck, and extremely politely asks "Mr. Cassady" if he could take his picture.

Turns out he's one of the big-wig photogs in this here Bloomingsville, Jeremy Hogan, shoots for the main local paper and a buncha national magazines n such, helluva nice guy, with that Midwestern humbleness that us coasters don't get to meet very often. In fact, he was *so nice* in his soft-spoken intelligence, I offered the option to hang with us if he wanted. Plus he was a local, and turned out to be an invaluable guide to the lay of the land where the land laid low.

Boom-biddy-boom we hit The Road, and before we got about ten feet from the theater, there were two bona fide college babes sitting side-by-side on a bench . . . reading (!) . . . *Naked Lunch* and Dylan's *Chronicles!* What?!?!

After our trio's silent passing with unified glued eyes, Cassady affirmed, "Yeah, we're in the right place."

Jeremy kept saying he thought he knew me. I get that sometimes, and most times there's no rhymes or reasons. But he kept going on about it, even though I'd never set foot in Bloomingsville in my life. Then he started to ask if I ever performed in New York, and I began to think maybe he knew sumpthin I didn't. A while later he frowned and asked if I ever sat in with David Amram ... and now I knew he was onto something. A day or so later he emailed me a photo he'd taken of me on stage with Amram at the Bowery Poetry Club in the East Village.

On stage at the Bowery Poetry Club in NYC.
Photo by Jeremy Hogan.

We did what we had to do while Walter did what he had to do, and looped back to the theater by sundown, and it was our local guide who knew exactly how far it was to each of the closest establishments. After plugging in all of our requirements he came up with this local brewery called Lennie's — where I was able to get one of those variety packs — you know — five different beers in different samplers — "Oh no! Brian's died and gone to heaven!"

And Boom — suddenly there was this krewe of John Cassady, Walter Salles, Jim Canary, Jermey Hogan and myself taking over the front corner of this amazingly cool brewery that local Jeremy told us was owned by this local restauranteur who had different places all over town and was sorta the local cool go-to guy.

Turns out, a couple years later, I'd meet this *other*

central Bloomington cat ... at Yasgur's Farm in
the Catskills of all places ... named the Wizard of
Wonder who knew and invited to his parties this very
restaurateur, Jeff Mease! And now years later we're all
in this big Prankster family together — but it was on this
first night at Lennie's in Bloomingsville that Jeff's space
became the central place for a buncha Beats to break beer
and bull the breeze together.

The director digging Cassady raps.

And when you get this kinda crew around a table it's electric. In this case it was a quartet, plus local Jeremy observing the unexpected out-of-town action. And although Jim Canary was the quiet Beatle, right away we had to ask him about the *On The Road* scroll, with the subterranean thought of sneaking into the Lilly Library late at night to look at it and soak in its magic, but sadly ol' Jim told us it was up in the owner Jim Irsay's office in Indianapolis.

The evening evolved into a rapid-fire trio of Walter, John & I alternately taking solos that the other two and four were raptured with, until another would grab the mic and flow it, with Cassady always the horse chompin' at the bit to get in, and he was definitely the lead player this night, with Walter and I trading off counterpoint solos, all of it filled with liquid laughter. Songs of Corso and Kesey and Weir and Coyote — everyone taking turns with some historical riff of hysterical importance with a captive audience cheering on the performer — we were our own best audience and held each other in the palm of our hands — Boom! over to you — Boom! over to you — tossing the story ball in a juggle of jams.

Walter riffed a long ode to the Coen brothers and how they kept the independent vision pure, and how he thinks Martin Scorsese is a God, but hasn't made a good film since *Casino*.

"*What!?*" I blurted. "You didn't like *The Aviator*?!?!"

"No," he said with a huge smile.

"You don't know what you're talking about!" I dismissed him with a wave, and we all laughed.

We also riffed on the power of filmmaker's film festivals where you can see multiple movies on successive nights by the same auteur. "It's like seeing the Dead do three or four different shows over successive nights," I said. "It's so much more expansive of the artist's vision than just seeing one show or movie."

"Yes, exactly," Walter riffs. "Their view of life. It cannot be expressed in a single show or film."

"Hey Walter," John says, "Thanks for inviting me to ride up in the Hudson with Garrett to the Beat Museum."

"You're welcome."

"I let Garrett do all the driving, he seemed to know that car pretty well."

"Yes. That was a good idea. Garrett has a bit of the Steve McQueen virus. He did most of the driving in the movie, and in fact he drove when we went out for three weeks doing the second unit shoots as well. The one thing that broke on the car was the speedometer. At some point, I think in Mississippi, we were pulled over, and the cop said to Garrett, 'Do you have any idea how fast you were going?' And Garrett said, 'No officer, please tell me. I don't have a speedometer.' And it happened to be 105."

"Whooooaaaaaa," roared the table.

Quiet Beatle Jim asked Walter about his first encounter with *On The Road,* and I hit the red button on my little digi recorder just in time: "I first read it when I was 18 or 19 — this was in the mid-'70s in Brazil, under a military regime, so there was censorship in the press, in all art forms, including literature, so the book wasn't translated in Brazil. It broke too many taboos to be translated in a conservative society like Brazil was then.

"I was immediately enamored by Dean and Sal and all those characters in search of all possible forms of freedom. And also, characters who were able to redefine their own future. This was exactly what we couldn't do at that time in Brazil. So the book and those characters became very emblematic to us. They were everything we would have liked to be, but we weren't allowed to pursue that. In fact, I reread *On The Road* before shooting *The Motorcycle Diaries* because I wanted to find that intensity it captures.

"It had a very unique quality because here were a group of young men and women, with Dean being the instigator of the journey," he said looking purposefully at John, "Who collided against a very conservative society — and *ours* was very conservative — and yet somehow they managed to create an enormous change later in the culture, and this is what we were aiming to do.

"I had the book in English, and at my university it went from hands to hands to hands to hands, and when it got back to me, at least 30 people had made notes in it!" as a gasp went up around the table. "And I still have that copy and cherish it. It echoed with a really large spectrum of people, and it reminds me of the line by Tolstoy which is that if you write about your own village it may end up being very universal. Kerouac was talking about what he had lived and experienced, and the urgency of that narrative, the honesty of that narrative was so resonant that 10,000 miles away we were deeply affected by it."

"Amen," blessed John.

"And so was the rest of the world. Rarely have I been in places where somebody doesn't ask me about *On The Road* — because they knew I was working on it — and they tell me, 'Oh, I was so touched by the book.' So there is something there. It may be because it is also one of the most resonant narratives about the passage from youth to adulthood, with all the pain that comes with it, and the moments of bliss that come with it, and the courage to find new frontiers. The fact that we're not accepting what is being offered to us, and every single generation has to amplify those frontiers, so the book was very universal and it resonated very deeply, and even hanging with you guys I still feel the same kind of impact as when I read it the first time. And Neal was responsible for that, John," he said directly to him, who got choked up and could barley mumble a "Thank you."

And after we'd solved all the problems of the universe and covered half the stories ever told, I knew we had a big day tomorrow and had to get to Columbus Ohio for the next screening. This party jam was just not ending, and I really love all my friends, and they were all having a good time, but Walter had shit to do. So I asked for the check … and when it came I picked it up and started waking to the cash register, guessing Walter was probably planning to cover us, but it was the only way I could get him away from the table.

"We gotta have a production meeting," I told him to a big grin as soon as he caught up to me. We wanted to all Road Trip together in my Blue Bomber . . . the three of us On The Road . . . but there was all this ... *reality* involved. He had to be at the Columbus theater at a certain time . . . all this shit there was no way I could confirm happening with me & Cassady at the wheel.

One thing that surprised me and was indicative of Walter's deep intelligence of so many things beyond cinema, he mentioned offhandedly that we needed to get to a state that voted the right way. The guy's from Brazil, and even *most Americans* don't understand the electoral college or who votes how, but Walter knew even from thousands of miles away how each of the 50 states voted in the Presidential election, and that Indiana had gone for Romney and Ohio for Obama. We didn't just have Jack in common — we could talk as in depth about politics as we could about film or Jack's spontaneous bop prosody (as Allen called it).

But the even cooler thing was — Walter & I had our first "production meeting." We both looked each other in unwavering eyes, stone cold sober after a long night of drinking, and worked shit out. He'd ride up with the I.U. film director Jon Vickers and the film canisters and I'd bring the beatnik badboy.

"See ya in Columbus."

Then — BOOM! The next morning, we were On The Road! And it was just the tip of the trip!

Me & Cassady on a nice four-hour drive for the first time in ages. It felt like the same kind of openness of unlimited time that Carolyn & I had living together. We got to tell stories by the hour — *because we've got hours!* Crazy tales of childhood ... or last week ... that we could riff for miles.

But first things first. Driving down to Bloomingsville on that little Hwy 37 from Indy I'd spotted a lingering Mourdock yard sign somewhere along the boulevard of the highway, and being the crazy politico I am, I had us keeping an eye out for it because it was going to be an historic political artifact! And sure as heck we spotted it, and I had to pull over on the highway and run and fetch it, John laughing his head off at my obsessive politicalness, and when I came running back he was standing outside the car waiting to capture the mad moment.

The political hunter captures his prey.

"How long were you at Carolyn's for anyway," he asked as we got back On The Road.

"Three months," I told him of my stay earlier that summer with his Mum in England.

"*Three months* ... holy shit, I had no idea."

"Yeah — it was crazy."

"I'll bet," he laughed. "You lasted longer than anybody."

"Yeah — and I was in your room! 'VAN MORRISON'S DRESSING ROOM!" I said with a laugh at the sign Carolyn snagged from backstage at one of Van's shows at the Royal Albert Hall.

John's bedroom at Carolyn's house.

"Oh yeah. He sure did love Jack and Neal. He and Carolyn became friends for a while. She knows everybody."

"For somebody who hated rock n roll, she sure did love her rock stars!" and we both laughed.

"What was the name of that Swedish guy?" John asked.

"Oh yeah . . . Ulf … something . . . *Ulf Lundell!* Yeah!"

"Right. That's it. Man, you're good, She found out he was playing in front of that classic Jack & Neal shot of hers from Russell Street projected on the screen behind him, and she went to bust him about it, and probably ask him for money, and I think he even gave her some, but he made a big fuss over her, so she forgave him and they became best friends," he said laughing.

"I got those signed posters he gave her laminated and hung in the front hallway."

"Nice job."

"Oh god — that was a funny story — *classic* Carolyn. So, as soon as I got there, she told me she wanted me to take all these posters in to London to get them laminated, right? So, the first time I went to that outdoor mall in Bracknell — oh yeah, I was getting your bike tire flat fixed."

"Oh yeah. Good thing. Good ol' Gets Things Done," and we laughed at his mother's nickname for me.

"Yeah, so, when they were actually fixing it — y'know, 'Come back in an hour,' — I went all around that outdoor mall area and actually made a list of every store that was there so I'd know what we had access to, y'know? And down at the end of this one walkway was this huge copy store, and right in the window it says, 'LAMINATING'! So, I go back and tell her that so I didn't have to haul the stuff all the way into London and back …"

"Right, right. Good idea. Geez, why didn't I think of that?" and we laughed.

"And so I come back and tell her, and that night we pull out all those tubes of posters from under her desk, right?"

"Oh yeah, she's got a ton of them under there."

"Right? So we go through 'em all, and there's all this different stuff — that Neal poster with his Joan Anderson letter words making the face … and a whole buncha different Kerouac things, and the signed Ulf posters, and all this crazy shit she'd collected for years."

"Right, right, yeah," he says laughing, thinking of all her cool stashes.

"So, finally, it got down to — I was leaving in a couple weeks, so I said, 'Ya gotta give me those posters to laminate for you,' y'know, cuz I didn't know which ones she wanted done. So I'm there at the dining room table and she comes in and just plops this whole armful of poster rolls down on the couch. So … okay … so, I take 'em into town the next day, and y'know, get to the store, and the posters are a bit of a pain in the ass, cuz first of all, they're huge, and second, they've all been rolled up forever, so they sorta stay rolled up when you take them out of the tube, right?"

"Right, right, ha ha."

"So I have to go over everything with them, and make <u>sure</u> they do it right, cuz y'know, God forbid they come out crooked or creased or something!"

"Right? She'd kill you!" and we both laughed.

"Yeah, cuz they're all one-of-a-kind and signed to her and everything."

"Yeah, I remember those."

"So, we go through all of them at the store, and I'm supposed to come back in a few hours, and I'm really nervous, cuz even if *they* screwed them up, *I'd* get blamed," and we both laughed. "But they did a great job!"

"Oh, good. Phew — that was close," and he laughed.

"But now I've got this enormous stack of posters, that are actually heavy and slippery — all these big three foot square posters, right? And they're all different *sizes* n shit. So it's this really unruly, stack, plus there's all the empty poster rolls, and I couldn't let anything get damaged, y'know?"

"Right, right," he laughs.

"So I finally get one of those mini-van taxis they have there ..."

"Oh, I love those things," he chimes at the memory.

"I balanced them in my hands like a pizza the whole winding way back home around all those crazy roundabouts and insane roads that were laid out by a chipmunk or something in the 5th century," and he's howling at the memory of the Le Mans rally race around those narrow roads driving on the wrong side of the street, "And my whole body's flying all over the back seat like I'm not strapped in on some crazy rollercoaster but all the time I'm holding this huge stack of slippery plates perfectly flat in front of me. Then I finally get home, and call out, 'Hi, I got the posters!' 'Oh, goody!' I hear from her bedroom, and she comes down the hall with this big smile on, and then sees all the posters on the dining room table, and goes, 'What's this?' 'The posters you wanted done.' *'I didn't want all these done.'* 'Well . . . that's what you gave me.' 'What *are* these things?' And she starts looking at them like she's never seen them before!" I laughed at the memory. "Y'know ... she goes, 'I hate this ...' and slides it away with a flourish. 'Oh this is *ugly* ... bin it,' she says. 'Why did you ... I thought you ...' 'I was just doing what you gave me.' 'Yeah, but I didn't want *all this.'* Finally she sees the ones she really wanted, and thank God they looked okay! But all these hoops me and the people at the store and cabbie and everybody went through getting these this job done and home safe and everything and she throws about half of them out! Of course I rescued them and put them in the garage or someplace. Oh MAN that garage! The vines hanging down from the ceiling!"

The front hallway of the queen's castle.

"Yeah, hell I wouldn't go in there without a lion-tamer's whip and chair!"

"Oh yeah, that was another thing I did when I was there, man. I went in with a ladder and clipped them where they were coming in and pushed the stems out of the roof."

"That's great, man," he says, laughing, then thinking — "How did you ever come to go over there in the first place?"

"My mom had just died in September, a year ago, so suddenly I was free after all those years of taking care of her, and in the spring I finally went to the New Orleans Jazz Fest, which I wanted to do all my life, and it was amazing, of course, and I got this idea that I was gonna go to all these music festivals, cuz they're really cost-effective — you can see ten amazing bands a day on a bunch of different stages, and when I got back home, I wanted to go to Glastonbury — that's one of the other big choice ones I always wanted to experience, and I looked into it, but they take a year off every seven years so both the land and the staff can recover, and this was the 'off' year. I was thinking of going, but now I wasn't, so I called to tell her that I almost came over to see her but I would next year, and she was like, I don't know if I told you this, but she said, 'Oh, honey, I don't think I'll be here next year.'"

"She said that?"

"Yeah. So you gotta get over there, man."

"I'm working on it." John had gone over with a one-way ticket earlier in the year intending to just stay living with her forever and gave the wrong answers to the wrong customs officer at the wrong time and ended up being deported back home. His appeal was still inching through the courts when we were on this November trip, and thank goodness it got approved in a few months, after a close family friend, Judith Barnett, prepared a massive defense for him, so John got to go over and be with his Mum for the last several months, during which she was totally with-it the whole time, until one day she got sick and died within a week. But at least John — the light of her life — was there with her at the end, just as she would have wanted. (There's a nice story about all this later in the book.)

Judith had included in the appeal that these were people of somewhat historic import, and wouldn't ya know it, but the judge who ruled in John's favor wrote in the decision reverentially about "the Beat Movement" and clearly knew and respected what it was.

As John often says, "Thanks, Dad!"

It was the fact that he couldn't get over there — and that she thought (turns out, correctly) that her expiry date was next year — which prompted me to hop the pond and spend those months with her.

"Bless your heart for going over there. I know she really appreciated it . . . even if she bitched about it sometimes," and we both cracked up.

"Oh man, New Orleans — I love that place!" John said. "'Crazy' Jerry Mitchell and I bought a 1956 Chevy panel truck in Berkeley in 1972, and headed off to visit his mother in Montgomery, Alabama, after his Air Force colonel father passed away. We were so broke, we put an ad in the *Berkeley Barb* or *San Francisco Oracle* or something for a rider with gas money. Some kid showed up with a $20 bill — good enough in those days — and we threw him in the back on the mattress, and took off. He was from New Orleans, and when we got to Lake Charles, we let him off to hitchhike the rest of the way to New Orleans since we were heading East to Alabama. He said, 'What? Aren't you going to Mardi Gras!?! I just assumed that that's why you came all the way down here from the Bay Area! Fat Tuesday is next week.' Jerry and I looked at each other with wild surprise and said, 'OK!' He ended up putting us up in his various friend's houses for two weeks in the French Quarter. I had the time of my life.

"On our way back to California, we laid up in Oklahoma City, out of gas, out of funds, and pretty much destitute. No tornadoes, mind you — that would have perfectly sealed our fate. With our last dime, I called mother Carolyn, and she wired us $20 for gas money, bless her heart. Western Union took about eight hours back then, so we had to wait a while. In the meantime, Jerry seduced this cute little maid at the motel where we were parked. She sneaked us a newly-cleaned room so I could shower, while they fooled around next door, and she gave us a whole tray of sandwiches, which lasted us all the way to LA. What a gal! There IS hope for mankind!

"We left the next day, with a full tank and all the sandwiches we could eat — life was good! But Jerry and I didn't get along so well after that — he was loco — so he dropped me off at my friend's house in LA and split for Oakland. I was more or less homeless, but glad to be rid of him. What an adventure THAT was!

"I ended up staying with a friend in Hermosa Beach for a few days. Funny story about her — we crossed paths over and over through the years, all across the country, even in Tuscaloosa, Alabama — crazy karma. We were born on the same day, September 9th. Meant to be? Oh well, she's married now. Saw her in S.F. a few years ago — bittersweet reunion. I eventually drifted back up north to Santa Cruz."

"Man your stories sound like your old man's stories!" I told him. "You come by it honestly, Cassady."

Arching from Indiana to Ohio —
Brother John with his camera at the ready.

"What's happening in Columbus, again?" John asked, never really a stickler for details.

"There's an *On The Road* screening at 4:00 . . . then there's some private party reception deal at somebody's mansion."

"Alright . . . well . . . I'm only gonna put up with this shit for so long."

= * = * = * = * = * = * = * = * =

We got to the Wexner Center for The Arts on the Ohio State University campus, and wouldn't you know it, but there was a massive Annie Leibovitz photo exhibition going on! — including the entire "Master Set" of all her 150 definitive shots — the first time it was ever all displayed in one place at one time before.

We were sufficiently early, and had seats reserved in the 7th row, so Johnny & I were able to soak in a bunch of Annie's juicy Jerry shots and get lost in her worlds. A couple years later I got lost at her house. It was that summer of 2014 when the Kesey Bus came to Yasgur's Farm (that story's also in *How The Beats Begat The Pranksters!* — geez, this is gettin' weird!) anyway, after that whole thing, I went to visit the woman who I first moved in with in New York City in 1980, Susan Ray, the young & babicious widow of the film director Nicholas Ray, who wrote & directed *Rebel Without A Cause,* among many others. There was some Astor mansion nearby along the Hudson River that I wanted to check out and sit on the riverbank and do some post-Woodstock writing. When I came back from the river to the closed under-renovation mansion, I talked to some cool artisan there about the estates of the Hudson Valley and all the different styles and eras that color the landscapes behind the trees, and he happened to mention that Annie Leibovitz lived right next door. WHAT?!?!

I'm nutty for her. She took that naked John Lennon wrapped around Yoko Ono photo just hours before he was killed — and about 10,000 other photos I just frickin' loved. And Boom! She lives *where?!*

So, I found her driveway, wove into the woods, and eventually came across an expensive large electric gate ... that was sitting open! Okay! ... Drive through . . . more woods . . . until suddenly! — there was some fantasyland Harry Potter-type structure . . . !

And I just roamed all the hell around . . .

Annie L's hobbit home.

But here we were now in Columbus Ohio with walls full of her — one of the artists who most graphically captured our culture beginning in 1970 — showing in the same space as an artist who so vividly captured the prior decades to 1970.

"She came out to our house in Los Gatos," John told me when we couldn't decide what to look at next. "*Rolling Stone* did that huge story on 'Neal's Ashes,' and the woman writer came to the house and hung out for a couple of days, can't remember her name. Then the next week they sent out a photographer — and it was Annie Leibovitz! I couldn't believe it!" he laughed. "She was already in every issue in those days. I thought she was as big a rock star as the people she was shooting. She took a picture of me standing in the window, but it came out really dark in the magazine. I look like a ghost hovering there. I've still got the issue at home. And still have my subscription. Never gave it up since I started it in the '60s."

"Oh yeah — I remember that piece. It's in *The Rolling Stone Book of The Beats*. I don't remember the picture, though. That was back when they were still writing, like, 10,000 word articles! Crazy times, man!" But by *now* it was about time for a movie!

This was now the *fourth* time I'd seen *On The Road* on the big screen! And it hadn't even been released to theaters yet! By now, the whole soundtrack — dialog and all — played like a familiar uptempo symphony in my head that I could pretty much dance to.

I've written three other pieces about it in *How The Beats Begat The Pranksters*, so there's no sense going into the movie, but one thing that struck me on this viewing was The MUSIC. The original score by Gustava Santaolalla, but also Dizzy and Bird and Ella and Son House and Coleman Hawkins . . . .

Plus, I'm visually oriented, and there's SO much to *see* in a Walter Salles film that really you can only catch on the big screen. He and I talked about this more than once — how the art he's creating is made for 50 foot wide canvases. In the past, it was bad enough that people were watching movies on 26 inch TV screens — now they're watching them on 4-inch phones! Drives him nuts. And sitting in front of his canvas I totally get why.

But also, ol' Johnny's a musician, plays everything from Ray Charles to the Grateful Dead, and we'd been playing nonstop jazz and Dead all the way to Columbus, so my ears were really ready for the audio saturation in a high-end theater of the Bebop masters set to a story I was rather fond of. And it delivered! If this movie woulda ended up being a hit, the soundtrack album woulda been killer!

So then it ends, and we head to this party, and ol' Johnny & I, well, we do our best.

And sometimes our collective best ain't quite good enough.

We got ourselves so fuckin lost we ended up on the wrong end of town! I mean, we were just so high. Not just from the whatevers, but simply being together … and being On The Road, and seeing *On The Road*, and hanging with the guy who finally made it, and being treated like "rock stars" as John would regularly reference.

But here we were — lost as shit — on the far wrong end of town — just *blazing* in a bliss of Beatific Beauty.

We finally used a Street Shout-Out and called somebody over and eventually found our way to the little lane a million miles away that was about as hard to spot as Annie's driveway was, and drove down this tiny dead-end road until there became a line of parked cars turning this "road" into a one-lane nothing . . . but there . . . through the trees — Lights! Lots and lots of lights!

And of course we'd now made ourselves fashionably late and the party was in full swing, and it was all catered n shit, with all these artsy & successful people, and here's disheveled Johnny and I rolling in prolly reeking of weed and booze.

"Hi! We're here!"

"Is this food free?"

Boom! There's Walter! Boom! There's all these sharp-cut suits and fine-line dresses and fancy people looking like they're on TV in high-definition with perfect hair and makeup and colorful costumes everywhere. Proper black vested caterers were carrying around traysful of exotic goodies I have no idea what they were, but we found the bar and started making the rounds. It wasn't exactly your Beat-centric scene — "Were you part of this *On The Road Again* movie?" — and before long the three guests of honor had gravitated back into a trio.

I asked Walter about Francis Ford Coppola's role in the movie since he bought the rights to *On The Road* in 1979 and held them until he found the right director. It was someone from Coppola's Zoetrope who caught *Motorcycle Diaries* at a film festival in 2004 and saw the similarities with *On The Road*, and told Roman Coppola about it, who totally "got it," then told his dad who tracked Walter down. Obviously it was nowhere in Walter's head that he would ever make a movie of the unfilmable favorite novel of his, but suddenly Francis Ford Coppola was on the phone talking to him about it.

He said Francis was very generous with his time and helped with both the script and the final editing. During tonight's screening I noticed a painting on the wall inside Burroughs's house that looked like one of Carolyn's portraits, and Walter confirmed that was indeed an intentional homage by his production designer Carlos Conti, who'd also done *The Motorcycle Diaries*.

Knowing of Walter's background in documentaries, I asked him what he thought the best music docs were, and without hesitation he rattled off, "*Don't Look Back*" (his first go-to), and then in rapid succession, "*Stop Making Sense, Gimme Shelter, The Last Waltz, Festival Express, Woodstock* . . . oh — and *Spinal Tap*," and we all laughed.

Walter told me I looked younger than I did in Toronto a few months ago, then said laughing, "It's the Road, man. It's good for you," and we both beamed at the truth of it.

"Here's sumpthin you'll like, Mr. Director," I said. "At Woodstock '94 — I have a whole book written about it I'll have to get out one day — but I was in the backstage area — long story — but there was this quiet afternoon moment at some point when I looked over and there was Michael Wadleigh [the *Woodstock* movie director] standing all alone on a little rise looking over the endless field of people. I let him hang there a bit and gave him his space, then went over and told him, 'All those people are here cuz of **you**. . . . Not Richie Havens or Jimi Hendrix — that was just the concert. It was your movie that made 'Woodstock' what it is.'"

"Oh, that's great, I'm glad you did that," Walter said.

"Yeah, he was pleased to hear it. But he seemed to be in a kinda quiet reflective mood, so I just sorta left him to it, but I'm glad I got to weave that into his mix in the middle of the sequel."

And the whole time we're talking, our faces inches from each other in a locked-in trio in a crowded room, people had formed a circle around us and were quietly soaking in our every word.

John, Brian, Jon Vickers, Walter Salles.

After a while we broke up the band and went circulating again, and at some point as the night was winding down, I was asking around about some reasonable motel in town, and Walter overheard me and promptly offered to put John & I up at the hotel he was at, which, when we got there, turned out to be some sort of Ritz-Carlton / Four Seasons type place, many rungs above John & my usual digs. And dig it we dug.

The next morning he & I were out front having a blurry morning come-to ciggie, "Hurtin' fer certain," as Johnny put it, when all of a sudden he goes, "Hey — there's Walter!!"

And sure as shootin' there he was! Tussled hair and puffy eyes like he just woke up, shirt-tails flapping, scratching his head, wandering & lost looking around. "Where's some place to get eggs?"

Suddenly the trio was reunited! And his sleepy morning face at 10AM reminded me of something he shared about his mind being so active he can't use the computer at night because it sparks his brain activity too much to ever fall asleep. After he mentioned this, I noticed all the emails I'd ever gotten from him were indeed in the morning and never at night.

But now it was time to go On The Road — doin' the Recovery Shuffle through the abandon streets of downtown Waiting For Columbus. We was Willin' as long as our Feats Don't Fail Us Now. After wandering past the gorgeous modern Columbus Blue Jackets hockey arena, we found Walter his eggs in a place called, no kidding, Sunny Side Up.

Boom! "A Beat, a Prankster and a Director walk into a diner . . . ."

I pulled out my trusty digi recorder and asked Walter why it took so long for the movie to get financed. He said, "Movies of novels with a more impressionistic structure, like *On The Road,* do not fit into what people expect a dramatic film to be, and have greater difficulty finding money. People get frightened about the themes that are in there. It's hard to believe, but it's the reality. I thought as recently as two years ago that this was never going to get made. The only reason it did was because the guys at MK2 in France fell in love with it, it's as simple as that.

"Something I still have a hard time understanding," he went on, "Is how no American company ever financed the previous attempts. Francis tells the story that the first attempts [back in the late '50s] by Hollywood with Marlon Brando ended with Neal's death in a car accident. They were trying to insert this and make it a mainstream narrative in which the guy who trespasses frontiers and implodes taboos would be punished in the end. Neal was outside their comfort zone. The whole time, we were on a very very tight budget, to the point where we never saw the images that we were shooting."

"No dailies *at all?!*" I blurted.

"No. But I had been through that before with *Foreign Land*, where I only got to process the film two months after we shot the entire thing. But with *On The Road* it would have been very difficult anyway because we were moving constantly in search of the last American frontier that the characters were trying to grasp. We traveled 60,000 miles making it, which is a lot. But we opted for the small roads as much as we could, and this led us to find places we were not expecting to find. For much of it we travelled with a very small crew, more like a documentary. We didn't know where we were going to sleep the next night. We followed a route suggested by the book, but we went even further than that."

And we talked about making the documentary *Searching For On The Road* and how that led him to spend a whole day out in the mountains with Gary Snyder — so far out that the GPS stopped working. "Two highly inspiring beings, igniters of this generation if you will, would be Gary Snyder and Neal Cassady," he said looking right at John. "They were *so* different. But they both opened so many possibilities in very specific directions."

John chimed, "Carolyn always poo-pooed the whole Buddhist thing. She said she thought Jack was just faking it with all that stuff."

"I think what Jack took from Buddhism were elements that were closer to a form of Catholic humanism," said the director who'd thought about this a lot.

"One thing that stuck with me," Walter went on, "Was the fact that Jack wrote so many of his books under the impression that *On The Road* would never be published, and that he had failed. But he kept writing. He was so prolific, he wrote so many books before *On The Road* was ever published."

And we talked about shaping the scenes and finding the dramatic structure and essence within the book, but also his love of the thrill of creative "mistakes" and how he instilled an openness for improvisation among the actors on the set — or "co-authors" of the film as he called them — letting them create in character — like how the whole scene with the three women in the kitchen at Burroughs's talking about blow jobs was completely improvised by the actresses (Kristen Stewart, Amy Adams & Elizabeth Moss). "You create unique moments this way," he said.

"Man, *you woulda loved the Grateful Dead,*" I said of the band he never saw but wished he had. "They were all about improvisation and making mistakes in every song," we all laughed.

And we got talkin about the Dead, and he told us about interviewing Bob Weir who shared a story about being at an Acid Test and going out and finding Neal passed out in a car and thinking for sure he was dead … until he saw a finger twitch … and then more … and then he saw him fully resurrect back to life!

I asked him why that wasn't in the *Searching For …* doc, and he said, "I had to cut that together in ten days."

He shot it over five years and has 120 hours of interviews with a ton of major cats talking about Jack & Neal and *On The Road* and such, and we can all hope one day a nice long version of it appears.

"Making that **I bumped into the youngest 70 and 80 year olds I ever talked to,**" he said. **"They hadn't lost two things — their curiosity and their beliefs. And a third thing — their integrity**. It was incredible to talk to them. Lawrence Ferlinghetti, Michael McClure, Diane di Prima, Amiri Baraka, they all were very very generous. But Ferlinghetti wouldn't talk to me until after we went for a bike ride together for an hour and a half. I never had that requirement before."

"Amiri Baraka, who is a poet, but also a political activist," he said, looking at me, "He told me, 'For me, *On The Road* is a story about blue collar kids who collide against the culture that they're not allowed in. And it's the story of sons of immigrants.'"

"Huh," said this first generation immigrant in America.

"Immigrants are always on the margins," Walter went on. "It's a question of identity for all of us. It's a matter of making the center more tolerant than it is. When you are in motion and you leave your point of origin and go on the road you have a better understanding of where you come from and eventually who you will become, or who you allow yourself to become. This is why I was always attracted by road movies and the narrative of the road, because the characters take the road to re-baptize themselves, to offer themselves a second chance. This is also what immigrants do, and this is why artists who *are* immigrants are always talking about the margins."

"The book is so polyphonic in that there are so many different voices in it, but also how it is perceived by others. Everyone has a different take on it. You can sense that in Barry Gifford's wonderful *Jack's Book*. It seems like *Rashomon* there are so many different views of the same events. Every single point of view is different than all the others."

And he riffed on staying true to the linear story of *On The Road* or expanding beyond it. "Just as Jack himself had trespassed what had been lived and included what he had imagined, like taking from Bull Lee's experience in Texas and bringing it to New Orleans, the orgone accumulator, all of those things."

He confirmed that Kristen Stewart had been attached to the film since 2006 before she ever shot a scene of any *Twilight* movie, and that Viggo Mortensen had always been his first choice to play Burroughs. "I've been a fan of Viggo for so long, he's the only person I called, actually. At one point he was in doubt whether he could get away from something else, and I was in dismay because I didn't have a second option. There's one guy who I love personally and he would have done a great job, but he was doing a mini-series, and that was Tim Roth."

"TIM ROTH! — I LOVE that guy!" I screamed out.

"Yeah, you *should* love that guy, he's fantastic. He's a really cool guy. I think that Tim would have been a very different Bull Lee but a great Bull Lee as well."

I asked him about another favorite actor of mine, Terrence Howard, the jazz player whose apartment Sal & Dean go back to. "Why Terrence? Because he's a musician. He plays everything. The guy's a real renaissance man. He knew the sax, and he really got it. Garrett is a good friend of his, and he does _the best_ Terrence Howard imitation, by the way. Gustavo Santaolalla who did the music suggested him as one of the great actors who can also play music. I mentioned to Garrett that I'd love to have Terrence Howard, so Garrett made the introduction, and Terrence said 'Yes, with pleasure.'"

"Did he know the book?"

"Yes." And there was a director's dramatic pause. "It's simple — *everyone* in the film loved the book. And everyone on the crew, too."

"That's so great," John said with his trademark laugh.

"Amy Adams was another one who really wanted to be part of it. She's so good. And Tom Sturridge who played Carlo, he did a lot of research into Allen's early journals and found lines we could use. He'd ask me and then Jose [Rivera who wrote the script] if he could integrate it into the screenplay and Jose worked with him specifically to incorporate them."

"What about when Dean gets on the bus in New York — in both the novel and real life it was just Neal who got on the bus, but you put Carlo/Allen with him."

"It's the same situation when they went to Mexico," the storyteller told us. "They didn't just go the two of them, there was the third guy, Stan Shepard, so there's moments where you have to narrow the narrative in order to develop the main characters, and this is what was done in those moments. In all adaptations you're obliged to narrow down to a few characters as opposed to developing all of them as you could in a book. The decisions are always very hard to make, and some are very painful.

"I like *Go* a lot," he continued. "I had to get John Clellon Holmes in there even if it wasn't as much as I would have liked. I think Ann Charters is so right in giving him credit for being an important voice of that generation, but it's not one that people always remember."

"Yeah — people will go 'Jack, Allen, Bill, Neal,' then maybe 'Corso, McClure, Ferlinghetti' ...." I said.

"He gets skipped over every time," John jumped in. "He was so instrumental and he doesn't get his due."

"Annie says the beauty of that generation is that they were all so different and yet so brilliant. You've got to acknowledge the genius of Jack, the genius of Allen, of Neal, but you also have to incorporate and applaud John Clellon Holmes and Amiri Baraka and a lot of others."

"It's like a great sports team or a band," I metaphored. "If the players are really good, it brings everybody's game up."

"The Grateful Dead, man!" Walter said to a round of smiles. "It's not only Jerry Garcia or Phil Lesh, it's *the band*. Or the same thing with The Beatles where everybody's discussing which one was the greatest in the group. And for the Beat Generation, I think that you had a group of ten, twelve, extraordinary writers, it was like a big band."

"Right, right, they were pushing each other, each trying to top what their friend had created, just like John and Paul did after every song trying to top the other," I chimed.

"Yes, you're so right about this," Walter said. "When *Go* came out, everybody was a bit destabilized in the group because somebody had written and gotten published a really great book with the muse of what later became a movement, which was Neal," as he and John locked eyes with smiles.

I said, "There was a great line in one of Jack's letters or journals sometime after he finished the scroll and was having trouble selling it, he said, 'I'm going to have to work as hard at selling the damn thing as I did at writing it.'"

"That's perfect. And so true. Oh man — look," Walter said, pointing at his watch. "We've got to check out of the hotel."

"What time's your flight to Brazil?"

"3:00, but you have to be there early for the international flights."

"Okay, no problem," and off the trippy trio tripped.

A couple of pillars.

When we got back to the hotel we had about ten minutes to pull off the lightning round check-out. But we'd hardly checked in, so it was pretty easy.

As we headed for the door, John paused as he passed the fancy flatscreen TV. "Wow — this is the first time I ever stayed in a hotel and never even turned the TV on!"

Down in the outdoor car lobby John & I started prepping the Blue Bomber for the next leg of The Adventure — the drive to the Rock n Roll Hall of Fame in Cleveland for the big Grateful Dead exhibit. It was part of what prompted this whole trip. First, that Walter's screenings were *after* the election and not before — when I was single-minded focused on an Obama second term — but also that the Dead show was at the Rock Hall. I always wanted to experience the place and knew I'd hate to go there a few years down The Road and wish I'd been there for the Dead show. So the fact that I could link the Kerouac movie with the Dead exhibit was what made this Trip a must-do no-brainer.

Eventually Walter came down and all the pieces came together. "Cassady, Hassett and the *On The Road* director are finally going On The Road together!" I made sure the krewe knew.

He signed my copy of *The Scroll* on the same page as Carolyn & John — "For Brian, my great amigo, pal, road brother and eternal friend — you're the coolest 'Beat' companion I had on this long journey!"

And he meant it. A month later I was in New York for the big premiere there, and the night before the event, he wanted to go to dinner . . . with just me. The guy knows everybody in the world, and he was in Manhattan, home to half of them, and he wanted it to be just me and him. Then the next day for the premiere I got a message while I was looking at Kerouac's notebooks in the Berg Collection at the NYPL — "Would you like to ride up with Walter to the premiere?" (!) So that peaking night began with just me, his assistant, and the driver in the limo to the movie stars and red carpet flashbulbs. (That whole story's in *How The Beats Begat The Pranksters*.)

Cassady, Salles & Hassett On The Road.

But here we were in Oh-High-Oh for the first
time bona fidedly going On The Road, everybody talkin'
fast and over top of each other, chomping at the jam bit,
wanting to share and joke and riff every second we could
cuz we all knew the trio was about to come to an end. I
was rattling off any last questions I had about the film —
including finding out how some of the Marylou dialog I
didn't recognize came straight from the 30 hours of tapes
of her that Walter got from Luanne's daughter of both
Barry Gifford and Gerry Nicosia's interviews — and John
was throwing in comic asides and laughing at his own
jokes the same way Henri Cru or Ken Babbs did — and
that Bomber was pretty electric bluegrass in the blazing
afternoon sun in the November of breadbasket America.

At the airport my digi recorder captured Walter
saying to John & I, "To get to the end of this tour, to be
able to share and talk about the book and the movie, I

still have the energy to do it, but sometimes I don't have it anymore, because I'm just too exhausted, there's no oxygen left, but the fact that you guys came for these four days, changed the nature of this trip, and the fact that it was at the end, I'm leaving with more energy than I had when I came in, so, thank you, thank you. I love you guys. And bless you for that letter to Garrett," he said of something John & I had written the actor who played Neal after some unfortunate press appeared. "I know that there was a co-authorship there, and I'd like to really thank you from the bottom of my heart. You made such a great difference to a guy who was hurting, and I hate to see someone with a great spirit hurting."

There were long hugs all around, all three of us getting choked up after days of heavy bonding and a lifetime in the same "family" having to now be broken up. He invited us to the premiere in New York next month which alleviated some of the separation anxiety, but we were all so glued to each other we watched as he walked down to the airport doors then turned one last time for a heartfelt eye-lock before he changed hemispheres.

It had been such a nonstop whirlwind of fun and screenings and vibrant conversations . . . as soon as he was Off The Bus, "the room" got very quiet for a minute, and I just drove John and I into the parking lot of the closest hotel next to the airport, pulled into a spot, turned off the engine, went "PHWWOOOSHH! What was THAT?!" and we cracked up in the joy of crazy Road madness.

We both had to get out of the car and pace the puck around a bit and crack some cold ones from the cooler in the bright blue-sky afternoon — cuz for the first time in days we didn't have ANYthing we HAD to do — so we just riffed the shit out of the moment!

"Can you believe he said he didn't even know *how to use* a green screen?!" I said of Walter's filmmaking.

"I know! The guy's so authentic it hurts!" John laughed.

"And I loved that story about him going into the meeting with the French investor guys to pitch *other* book ideas, and it was almost an afterthought to bring up *On The Road*!"

"Yeah, right?! That's a movie in itself right there!" John laughed s'more.

"And I love how he kept talking about creating 'unpredictability' . . . "

"He's like the Grateful Dead of movie-makers!" John said laughing. "No wonder I like the guy!"

"Yeah and how he said the actors used basically no makeup the entire movie — that he didn't want it to be 'a movie star movie' ... even though it ended up being full of movie stars!"

"He's the perfect guy for this."

"Your Mum told me though about how Jack and Neal would *always* have a comb with them, and always kept their hair looking perfect."

"Oh yeah, I forgot that."

"You never see a picture of them with messy hair — except that one time Jack came down off the mountain and Gregory messed it up for the *Mademoiselle* shoot."

"'Every girl crazy 'bout a sharp dressed man,'" John sang, then sounded out the riff.

"Ya gotta look the part if ya wanna score the role."

"Or even just score," he said, laughing.

"Oh, another thing that was amazing was he said almost everything in the movie was a first take! Can you believe that?!"

"No!" he laughs. "But it looks that way. It's all so spontaneous. Just like Jack and Neal. He really captured that. It felt like home movies."

"Yeah, in a way he sorta captured a Robert Frank thing, or the Maysles brothers or something, cinema vérité, like — chaos with a camera rolling. Like that song in the back seat of the car! That that guy completely improvised that and just started singing it. And he said Kristen was so touched by it she was holding back tears, and you can see it in the shot, and that it was just one-take!"

"He's amazing. Carolyn's gaga over him even if she didn't love the movie," John said.

"I KNOW! I asked her if she was ever in love with anybody again the way she was with Neal, and she says, 'Yeah, Walter Salles.'" (!)

"Really?! ha-ha-ha. I didn't know that, but I believe it."

"He's just such *a nice guy!* And he's so fuckin *smart!* Shit! English is his second or third language and he has *a bigger vocabulary than I do!* I hate 'im!" I said.

"And how 'bout that house party?! He sure knows

how to work it. And that hotel room last night?!?! Nicest place I've stayed in a while! Who is this guy?! ha ha ha," he said as we hoisted cold green bottles under bright blue skies in the yellow afternoon sun.

"Alright man, should we hit it? Go see Jerry at the Rock n Roll Hall of Fame?"
"Let's do it."

And whaddya know but just as we're drivin' outta the *On The Road* town to the home of rock n roll — what should our signpost up ahead be?

"They even spelled it right, ha-ha-ha," Cassady says with pride. "Wait'll Mum sees this!" as he snaps away for Family Pride Day.

We jumped back in the Bomber and clapped the board — **The Road, Take 2**.

"I gotta tell ya," John began, "When I first heard about this Rock n Roll Hall of Fame thing, I was pretty skeptical. 'You can't put rock n roll in a museum for god sakes!' But when we came with Kesey in '97, it was a Blast! He called me up in Santa Cruz while I was doing the dishes one night and told me he got a letter from the Rock n Roll Hall of Fame and that they wanted to induct The Bus! And he wanted me to drive it there 'because your dad can't make it.' Great line — never forgot it."

"Nice!" I said, "That was the first major show The Hall ever put on there. I thought it was so cool and perfect, and I was like, 'This thing's gonna be *Great!*' I mean — they were *starting* with the coolest part of the sixties, ya'know? Obviously the best decade for music."

"No kidding!" he laughs. "It was called 'I Want To Take You Higher'! Great name for it. There was a bunch of them there that day — Donovan! ... Country Joe ... Big Brother ... and *we took over* the stage," he said, laughing s'more. "Babbs on his trombone ... I think we played *Gloria* ...."

"You guys *always* played *Gloria!*"

"Yeah, that's true," he laughed. "When we drove in from Chicago, just before we got there, Kesey tells George [Walker] to the pull The Bus over and I got to drive right up onto that concourse plaza thing they have out front ... and we were just *mobbed*, man!" he laughs. "This *sea* of teenyboppers just *swarmed* us. I was afraid I was gonna *kill* somebody. It was a madhouse!" he laughs. "People were passing us joints all over the place, and there was an open bar for the performers that we totally raided. There was nuthin but empties by the time we were done with it," he laughed loud.

"Did you go in the museum itself?"

"Yeah. I don't remember much. But they had John Lennon's Rolls Royce and Janis's Porsche — *that* I remember. Man, I'd love to drive those things. Neal would, too. (ha-ha) But he'd probably wreck them in an hour," he laughed. "Oh and they had the Sgt. Pepper costumes — the real ones they wore on the cover. *Those* were cool! Super elaborate — so many little details you could never see on the album."

"I hope they still have those. Love to see 'em. I wonder what they're gonna have on The Boys? [the Grateful Dead]" I longingly pondered.

"Pigpen's last wine bottle," he laughed.

"A roach from 710 Ashbury!"

"Jerry's sweatpants."

"Bobby's shorts!"

"The first cassette tape ever bootlegged!"

"A box of rain!"

"A wall of sound!"

"A Tiger in a trance!"

"Oh yeah! I hope they have his guitars! I'd love to get a close-up look at the pick-ups and all that custom inlay," said the guitar player.

"I think Jim Irsay owns that — the guy who bought Jack's scroll. That's where we gotta go!"

"No kidding! I'll put a man on it!" and I cracked

up at his stock phrase.

"Speaking of valuable stuff — boy your Mum's house is full of it! The whole time I was there I was petrified I'd accidentally break something!"

"Yeah, I'll bet!"

"Like, *everything* in that house is worth about a million dollars, or at least she *thinks* it is."

"No kidding!" he laughs.

"I mean, everything dated back to her childhood, or the Jack & Neal days."

"I know — everything got a story. She's got a million of 'em," he laughed.

"I loved being there and everything, but I remember when I got in the cab to go back to Heathrow, I was like, 'Phew! . . . *I made it!* I didn't break anything!!'" I said laughing in the memory of it. "Oh, you know what she's still got that I loved — that Cassady mailbox sign from Bancroft! That thing is *so* cool!"

Mugshot of madness at Camp Carolyn.

"Oh yeah, she keeps it on the bookcases in the hall. I love that, too. And those books, man! She has thousands of them! I couldn't read 'em all if I lived to be a hundred!" John said.

"Oh yeah — this crazy thing happened . . . so, I was kind of systematically going through all those books over the three months, and she had one section of just England books, like, travel guides and stuff. And I saw this one about Famous British Eccentrics — oh god this is horrible — so I find this, and walk into the kitchen smiling away and go, 'Here's a book you should be in!' And I thought I was kinda paying her a compliment, ya'know? cuz she identifies as British and is as eccentric as hell ...."

"Right," he laughs.

"But I walk in there and show her this, and she looks at me with horror and just slams something down on the counter and storms out of the room!"

"Oh no!" he laughs.

"Yeah!! She was *super* pissed!" I said laughing at the memory. "I mean . . . she's an artist, a writer, she in relationships with two of the most eccentric people of the 20th century, she's 90 years old with posters of rock stars on her walls, and a waterfall in her back yard, and all these bizarre rituals — like, she can only go to the grocery store at 1:00 on a Wednesday, and all this weird shit — but *she sees herself* as this proper English aristocrat."

"Right, right," he's laughing.

"And I felt so terrible! Like ... her image of herself is so refined and 'by the book' ... and meanwhile she's talking about sex like she writes for *Penthouse Forum* then quotes Dickens in the next sentence . . . but no, she's not eccentric!" I laughed.

"Oh man — howja get outta that one?!"

"I for sure apologized, but I tried to point out how, y'know, she was *an artist* and spent her life in the theater and painting portraits and having movies made about her and was a member of that decidedly outsiders' Groucho Club over there and hung with Ralph Steadman and Jay Landesman and Allen Ginsberg . . . but '*No,* she wasn't *eccentric!*'"

"Much!" and we both laughed. "God bless her.

'Love you, Mum,'" he said by way of pond-hopping telepathy to her. (And for more on John & Carolyn's telepathy, check out "The Queen & The White Knight" in the next section, wink wink.)

And as the conversation kept swirling we kept whirling into Cleveland and found ourselves one of our go-to Red Roof Inns and had a not-pushing-it night and woke up in good time for a Rock 'n' Roll Grateful Day.

Blown away!

From the git.

I.M. Pei! All. The. Way!

What an architect! Holy spidoodlies!

Forget what's inside the building — the structure's worth the price of not paying the admission! A great towering glass pyramid on the edge of a Great Lake — with a cantilevered extension over the water like a stack of 45s waiting to drop onto a turntable — all set back from the huge open plaza where John drove Kesey's Bus . . . that today was filled with an army of steel drum players raising the Dead!

And right there — streaming across the pyramid facing the plaza were blazing the full-color words **"Grateful Dead"** . . . that have summoned so many to go On The Road so many times before.

Cassady at the pyramid.

As soon as we passed through the hallowed doors, we were hit with a sign — "PHOTOS AND VIDEO NOT PERMITTED" — and Johnny & I being the strict law-abiding types we are, followed this directive for about a minute.

And when we got home at the end of the day, we'd each taken *exactly* 100 photos! Not a vastly different number of shutter clicks each — but *the exact same number*! And it wasn't 99 or 42 or 53 or anything — it was *exactly* one-zero-zero on the old digi camera count! … We've been synched into sumpthin bigger than us from the beginning.

And immediately the giant creatures from Pink Floyd's *The Wall* came crawling out of the ceiling to grab us. This was not your grandfather's museum — this was an acid trip waiting to happen! And we were visiting with just the right band playing the soundtrack.

We took the elevator to the top (5th) floor and let the slippery slope begin. Right away — there was Pigpen's Hammond B3 and his beat-up congas ... Jerry's Rosebud guitar and Bobby's beautifully inlayed Ibanez ... Mickey's dancing skeleton drums ... old road cases with Owsley's original Steal Your Face stencils ... the giant original paintings of the front and back covers of *Live Dead* ... artwork gels from *The Grateful Dead Movie* animation ... Stanley Mouse's charcoal & ink portraits of the individual band members from *Workingman's Dead* ... Robert Hunter's original penciled lyrics to *The Wheel* ... Bill Graham's first permit to be a "Dance Hall Keeper" at the Fillmore in San Francisco ... the Western Union telegram confirming the Grateful Dead for the Monterey Pop Festival ... and on and on and on.

We were there for hours spinning in circles from one "You gotta see this!" to another "Oh my God I didn't know that!"

Turns out, John was a huge fan of the band from

the time he bought their first album as soon as it came out in 1967.

In our revelous reconnoitering of the multi-level architectural playground designed by-&-for people who live outside boxes, we came across an outdoor balcony space hanging over Lake Erie, and even more to our surprise and liking, it was right next to a little beer & wine bar! It was out there in the fresh smoky sea-&-beverage air that he told me the story of being in high school and hearing an announcement over the school P.A. to report to the principal's office. "Oh no! What have I done *THIS* time?"

When he got there, who should be leaning against the counter in the principal's office but his day-glo-costumed Dad with his similarly clad sidekick Ken Kesey wearing an American flag top hat and orange Beatle boots! "Ah yes, harrumph, well you see, we've got to take Johnny to a, uh ... dentist appointment, yes, that's what it is, a dentist appointment, the cornerstone of every good health program, you understand ...."

And waiting outside was none other than the original psychedelic school bus, probably making its first return to the purpose of its design since the Pranksters got their paint-covered hands on it. Off they whisked, John and sister Jami to some other high school down the peninsula where none other than the Grateful Dead were playing a high school dance!

Everybody remembers their first Dead show — but few have as good a first show story as "Neal's kid." He tells the tale in-depth in his Grate adventure-filled

Visions of Neal story collection, but I'll take the buzz of hearing it in person while hoisting some cold ones avec herbal remedies on the balcony of a building full of their history.

After our refresher course and refueling, we returned to the colorful dance, and sure enough, there was Lennon's Sgt. Pepper uniform; and ZZ Top's very custom Eliminator Coupe from all their videos and making us think of Jim Canary; and the CBGB awning from my beloved New York, and floor after floor of jaw-dropping gems that jazzed our jollies and juiced our jam.

But as much as we loved seeing Jimi Hendrix's drawings of rock bands, and Grace Slick's sexy stage-wear, these two old Deadheads kept returning to the rooms where their music was blaring. Eventually in one of them we found a whole display on John's dad! And another on just the Acid Tests — including audio recordings of Neal rapping from stage.

One of the little interpretive signs read — "The way Cassady approached life, *'something between philosophy and art,'* as Jerry Garcia said, profoundly influenced the direction of the Grateful Dead for the band's entire existence."

And I flashed back to Walter Salles at breakfast yesterday saying Neal was the igniter of the generation . . . and here he was on the wall of the Rock n Roll Hall of Fame . . . applying to a whole other generation . . . a whole other context . . . a whole other world.

Jack Kerouac and Allen Ginsberg were the primary main voices of the Beat Generation . . . and the Grateful Dead were the primary voice of the psychedelic generation that followed . . . with the Merry Pranksters the connecting tissue between . . . and **it was the same singular person who is cited by all three as their muse and driving force.**

Who the hell else in history in any creative medium in any century can claim such a distinction?

But Cassady, Cassady, Cassady . . . .

Part Two

Carolyn Cassady

and The Downhome

6

First Meeting &
First Bonding
with Carolyn

Here's an account, originally published in The Hitchhiker's Guide to Jack Kerouac, *of my first meeting Carolyn Cassady, and subsequently becoming friends.*

Event: The climatic Saturday night of the "On The Road Jack Kerouac Conference"

Date: July 31st, 1982

Location: Boulder, Colorado

Written: February 2013

Published in: The Hitchhiker's Guide to Jack Kerouac

Of course, for the final big event everyone came early and was milling about — including The Holy Trinity of Yin — **Jan Kerouac, Carolyn Cassady, and Edie**

Kerouac Parker — each a sun in her own solar system of friends and fans.

Jan was 30 years old at this point. She didn't much want to be on panels or in the spotlight or anything and the only real appearance she made was at one of the group readings to riff from her first and just-published semi-autobiographical Kerouacian book *Baby Driver*.

She was shy and quiet. But stunning! I mean — gorgeous! A tranquil beauty. Thin, in tight jeans, with this super pretty tanned face and blazing light blue eyes, a to-melt-for smile, and cute shoulder-length jet-black hair. Almost Liz Taylor-like. Or a young Jordana Brewster in more recent movie star casting.

Like many conference participants, this was her coming out party in Beatlandia. Besides being her first tentative step into the public arena, it was here in Boulder that she first learned from local Buddhist student and author John Steinbeck IV, the son of the novelist, that children are entitled to half of their parent's royalties, something she never knew or collected on before.

She always had a bevy of boys around her, and in my own young Canadian stranger-in-a-strange-land shyness I was too goo-gooed to go talk to her. Cuz also it was so weird ... you love this writer in a dude-to-dude hero mentor teacher master artist way — but suddenly here he was manifested ... as a babe! It was this weird thing of being attracted to this girl who was really ... *your dad*. I know. Crazy. You couldn't take your eyes off her — she was hot as hell — but ... she was also ... *Jack*.

And if that wasn't freaky enough! It was kinda the same thing with **Carolyn!** — except she was 59 years old at the time — but still intimidatingly gorgeous! Like a Sophia Loren, or maybe Grace Kelly if she'd lived; skinny, and blond, with a striking model's face and the cutest little dimples when she smiled; calm, and regal, and beatifically glowing, with twinkling eyes, and confident, and at peace. You sure knew why the ol' Beat boys fell for her! And ditto every cowboy at this rodeo!

I could start talkin' to Ginzy or Kesey or Huncke or just about any of these guys real easy, but sometimes I'm more Jack than Neal when it comes to jaw-droppingly beautiful girls. And to her lucky genes and healthy living credit she was probably the most attractive woman in the whole scene — while simultaneously being the oldest. When I was lucky enough to meet her again years later, I was well over the insecure shit and made damn sure I made up for my youthful Boulder bashful shyness and went right up and became friends and remained so until the day she died.

On the back garden deck at Camp Carolyn in England.

The thing is about Carolyn ... she was consistently attractive from the time she was a girl. This was both a blessing and a curse, as it probably is for all who win the good looks lottery. Just go ahead and try to find a heterosexual man who met her who didn't have a crush on her. You'll spend your life in vain.

How we first ended up arm-in-arm was somewhere in the '90s, at the Algonquin Hotel in Midtown Manhattan. Besides having met in Boulder and then elsewhere, like everyone else I'd been enamored with her since first reading Jack's descriptions. And to finally meet her! Crazy, man! I mean, it makes no sense. There was definitely an attraction ... but it wasn't about sex. She was hot — and also jazzman cool. She was petite, but loomed so large! She was Marilyn Monroe — but she was ... *my mother!* It was nuts! Positively Oedipal. Probably untreatable. But she was totally unBeatable!

So, we're down in a dark Dorothy Parker booth in the spirit-filled Algonquin lobby bar with Doug Brinkley, John Sampas, David Amram, and others hovering, then a few of us finally cut out and up to a top floor suite that one of the Greeks from Lowell had rented and continued the party up there with the big old windows that slid right up, and jazz playin' from a radio station, and drinks pouring, and big rooms to roam around in, and crazy late-night confessions and gossip. And after another round or two of this madness, Carolyn finally leaned in and whispered to me she was ready to go back to her room.

We'd bonded throughout the night to the point that she wanted me to be the one to walk her home. And so, the two of us left the party, this very odd couple, tottering down the hall, walking in a formal elbow arm lock like that first shot of her & Neal together on the streets of San Francisco, except drunkenly swaying on this lurching ship all the way to her cabin door, me freaking out that I'm in the Neal & Jack slot, but also playing with the moment, and we're having a hell of a time laughing at whatever was happening, and it hit me — *that's the exact same laugh Neal and Jack heard!*

She was around 70 at this point, and a lot about her had evolved — her brain, her body — but one thing that doesn't change about people is their laugh. And she

had the most wonderful childlike joyous giggle. I loved
it. And when I love a girl's laugh, I make sure I hear it as
often as I can. So I'd make her howl till she was gasping!
It was great!

And all of that was born this Algonquin night. And
when we got to her door — what did I do? Guess before
you read on. What would you do? . . .

You know what I did?

I took her hand and kissed it, like an old-school
English gentleman. Little did I know at the time she
had a real thing for English gentlemen! — and in fact
had moved there a year after the Boulder summit! But
I let it go at that noble gesture. "Well, wasn't this a
WONDERFUL night!" she gushed in unfiltered joy. A
gentleman not insinuating himself on her, but rather just
joying in the joining of each other's company. "We're all
just walking each other home," as Ram Dass put it.

And that's what she & I did for the rest of our life.

7

Happy B Day to The Big C!

*My Mother and Carolyn were born one week & two
years apart . . . and died one week & two years apart.
This birthday poem was a retrospective of some of
the many moments and memories of our Adventures
together. The whole family loved it, and it got
recirculated many of her subsequent birthday seasons.*

Event: Carolyn Cassady's birthday
Date: April 28, 2008
Written: April 2008

A girl so nice you had to C her twice!
It's the Big Sea at Big Sur!
And finding the sacred rocks to reflect,
and seeing the glistening gems shine thru
the crashing waves of life
with you.

I saw the best minds of my generation buzzed on wine
coolers before breakfast!
The only ones for me are the mother ones, the ones who
laugh and live, and live to laugh, never mum to talk,
but always winking in the immensity of it, desirous of
everything at the same time, the ones who never yawn
except when it's really really *really* late, who burn, burn,
burn like fabulous yellow van Gogh paintings exploding
across the sky, and in the middle we see your face and
everybody goes, "Awww!"

There she is!
Mother Earth!
Mother Mirth!

Who taught me courtesy
while pushing curiosity;
and how to laugh
while grounding me
in eternity;
and about my own Taurus mother,
and the joys of inter-generational Adventure Fun,
which I brought home and shared and we thrived and we
laughed and I thank you.

Boy, do I miss those living rooms full of time,
and glasses full of wine,
and laughing so loud
we had to turn it down,
and driving and "oh goshing" all around
that San Francisco town
and even being Europe bound!

From the Algonquin's table,
yet another round;
to loving glances
with clinking glasses
on police station steps
as we stay out of step
with the stomping classes,
dancing in the eternity
of the songs and the stories that echo forever.

Thanks for caring, and thanks for sharing
a life that's rife with light at night;
You've held my hand across more than an ocean,
in a rainbow of color
that seemed to come from above.
But you said,
"It comes from within."
And that's why I love you!

Mighty Teacher!
Mighty Mother!

Mighty cool you're still shining today!

Muchos love from the universe, sweet angel!

Brian, Sweetie –

You are, as I keep saying, just too much.
You take the cake as always. It is so comforting to
have such a friend who has this outrageous view of
me — I'll take it.
I do think of you and all your creative energy
so often— relive Amsterdam and CA when you
brightened my life.
Brian gets things DONE. And done beautifully.
I love you,
CC xxxxxxxx

Oh, Brian...

I just read your poem ... I sat here crying!!

It was just so perfect ... and so right on ... Thank you
so much for that!
XXOO
Jami Cassady

Brian —
You did it again!
Best one yet, my brother-from-anuthr-mother!
Come back and visit us sometime!
All best,
John

8

The Royal Woods of Cassady County

Right after I arrived at Carolyn's in England on June 6th, 2012, I immediately fell in love with the winding road thick foliage park area where she lived. When I mentioned this in an email to brother John, he told me the backstory of how it was part of a giant wildwood preserve. Carolyn told me a little more about it, and I suddenly saw the ancient trees as a living metaphor of the person I was living with.

Date Written: June 2012
Location: Warfield Park, England

Tiny me by giant tree.

All the king's horses and all the king's men
Rode through these woods and back again

They cut down the trees all over the land
But chopping this forest was strictly banned

The king must have his galloping grounds
And live surrounded by chirping sounds

So over the centuries these trees grew
Preserved and protected from anything new

Above me now in the wind they sway
Living history — like with whom I stay

As old as the hills with stories to tell
They whistle and wink and spark a spell

Maybe they creak but they're still here
Wondrous company to share a beer

It's the land of the aged, well preserved
But flowing freely, unreserved

Branching wider every day from birth
And deeply rooted in mother earth.

9

A Shakespearean Cassady

Event: Historically heavy rains in England
Date: June 2012
Location: Carolyn's house, Warfield Park, England

A month of rain in 12 hours
can't dampen the Spirit
of a lifetime of experience
or the experience of a lifetime.

Two compatible souls a generation apart,
Somehow related, somehow unjaded, somehow not
faded,
Still giggling unburdened, still freely unherded,
Two jazz cats still flowing, still riffing, still reading
the mind of the other.

Tis a play devoutly to be wished,
On Shaky Willie's garden stage,
Halfway around the Globe,
In a comedy of the present and a tragedy of age
Where laughter is the direction and wine is the line.

10

Haiku For Carolyn

*These are not traditional 5–7–5 haiku — they're
what Kerouac called Western Haiku — "simple 3-line
poems that make a little picture" — written while
I was living with and inspired by Carolyn. There
certainly was something about that woman that
inspired. She had so many arts flowing through her
at every given moment — painting, writing, theater
— it couldn't help but transfer to those around her.
This blooming, sketched over the summer of 2012, is a
portrait of her, using a tiny haiku brush. Everything
comes directly from something she said or I saw.*

*Event: Living with Carolyn in England
Location: Warfield Park, Bracknell Forest
Written: June – August 2012*

Portrait painter, married Adonis
loved a movie star
could still draw their faces from memory

Houseful of books
skyscraper stacks
grow on every surface

Still watches movies
like the set and costume designer
she always was

Still cooks every meal
meat, potatoes and veggie
like her biochemist father taught her

Touch-typing emails
looking at giant Mac screen
words flow with ease

In love with history
so much a part of it
and not just this lifetime

Designed her own garden
and put in a waterfall
knowing I was coming

WACed a war
mothered a family
batted away suitors by the battalion

Hung with heavies
but keeps it light
as fans gush their hearts

Still twinkles by day
and beams by night
reading in every morning

Turquoise and purple
color her home
herself, and her life

She enjoyed this life
as much
as she enjoyed all her others

At home in her home
her skin
her life.

11

The Queen
& The White Knight

*Written in the days following Carolyn's passing,
reflecting on the uncommonly powerful bond between
mother and son.*

Event: Carolyn Cassady's passing
Date: Carolyn & son John's entire life together
Location: Everywhere they were
Written: Sept. 23rd, 2018

Ya know how our favorite Beats were not exactly role-model parents?

How there aren't a lot of heart-warming parent-child stories in Beatlandia?

Well . . .

there *is* one.

Carolyn Cassady and her son John were sumpthin else.

Honestly I'm tearing up now just picturing them together.

It was the greatest thing.

They loved each other as much as two people can.

And they were like a comedy duo, like a Burns & Allen, Nichols & May, or Dashiell Hammett's Thin Man couple, wise-crackin' all the time — so in synch you'd think they'd been jamming since birth!

They had each other's rhythms and thoughts *down* — and could just *play* the other — it was amazing — like two instruments trading off in a band.

There could be a room fulla people and they could be in different clusters and they'd still somehow be hearing each other and one would say something and the other would laugh from 10 feet away.

And this was never ending. They didn't even have to be on the same *continent* and they could make each other laugh — just by hearing the other's voice in their head.

And they would tell the most risqué jokes or one-liners that would make me blush — and the two of them would just roar!

There were so many nights in hotel rooms or restaurants that we'd all be talking and laughing so loud there were noise complaints.

When I mention in my tribute to Carolyn about her inspiring me with my own mom, it was really seeing them *together* that exploded my framework of what a parent-child relationship could be.

They were like two little kids when they were together. Look at that selfie. I bet that's the exact same expression of giddy silly playful joy Carolyn had when she was 4 years old.

And they could also be like two complaining old fogies on a swing on the front porch grousing about how things ain't like they used to be — then crack each other up at the irony.

What I'm saying is — there was at least one tremendous parent-child relationship up on Mount Rushmore in South Beatlandia.

And those two were living it.

Author Billy Craddock (*Be Not Content*)
momentarily content next to Carolyn,
who obviously had a thing for rebel writers;

with John, Brian and sister Jami
— at John's 50th birthday celebrations,
September 2001, San Jose, CA.

12

Carolyn Cassady Tribute

The morning of Monday Sept. 16th, 2013, Carolyn woke up with a pain in her tummy, and went by ambulance to the hospital. Thank the Great Spirits that John was back there with her after an immigration snafu kept him out of the country for over a year. He sent out an email to the family that Monday night, and every few hours all that week. As the news was not getting better, I began reflecting on Life With Carolyn, and started writing some memories — in part to focus my mind and have something positive to show for some depressing days. As things continued to not improve, I knew at least I'd have something roughed out if our worst fears were confirmed — as they were that Friday, just four days after she took ill. I loved feisty old disciplined literate laughing Carolyn, and when someone I love dies, I need to write about them. When I posted my tribute to her on my website within probably an hour after receiving the fateful email from John, it quickly went "viral" as the kids say. Inadvertently, I'd ended up announcing to the world that this giant had fallen. The New York Times, L.A. Times and all sorts of places contacted me, and my Facebook feed exploded, and I guess the good news is I didn't feel alone, and ended up collectively mourning for days with thousands of people around the world. Here's what I posted that sad Friday night.

Date: Sept. 20th, 2013
Location: Bracknell, England
Written: Sept. 17th–20th, 2013

Another giant has fallen — another angel taken flight.

Carolyn Cassady has just left us to join Neal and Jack on that great road trip in the sky.

Her son John, the light of her life, was there by her side till the end. After a year's refusal of entry into the U.K., just 3 months ago he was able to return to England to be with her.

She was her regular rockin self up through Sunday, woke up with a tummy ache Monday morning, had an infected appendix, and checked out by Friday.

We should all be so lucky. She was 90 years old and still drank her white wine and smoked her More menthol ciggies every day.

That is to say — she was living the life she chose, on her own terms, in her own house, until the very end.

Besides Neal's love for her, it's my considered opinion she was also the love of Jack Kerouac's life — and they pledged to be together in the next one.

So there's that.

Carolyn was spiritual, an intuitive channel, naturally smart, well educated, well read, independent, creative, curious as all get-out, strong … yet loved hugs, was uncommonly forgiving while still holding a firm sense of right and wrong, and was a helluva gifted portrait painter. Sold hundreds of them.

She grew up in a library of a house, with a biochemist father and English teacher mother, and intellectual discourse and reading were the orders of the day.

She got her BA as one of the first students at the revolutionary Bennington College in Vermont, then earned her MA in Theater and Fine Arts at the University of Denver, where she was living when she met Neal.

Carolyn was the first of the then unnamed generation of Beats to move to San Francisco, and she was the reason Neal went there, which is why Jack went there ... and so tumbled the dominoes of history.

I used to phone her at her cottage home in the forest around Windsor Castle every few months just to chat, and a little over a year ago she told me she didn't expect to be here next year.

Since none of her three kids could get over there at that point, and I was sort of freed up for the first time with my mom having just passed, I went and lived with her for three months, and boy did we have a time!

When we first started hanging out in the '90s, we were having so much fun, it made me realize I could be doing this with my own mom, who was about the same age. And for the next 15 years my mom and I took our Adventure even further and were even better friends than we had been before — and it was thanks to Carolyn opening those doors wide so I could see how much possibility there was.

Carolyn was born a week after my mom in April, and died a week after her in September. I always wanted to get the two of them together but I guess we were always a week off. Talk about fabulous roman candles exploding across the stars — those two together woulda lit up the night sky until dawn!

And she wasn't just a surrogate mother to me, but was the den mother to the entire Beat Generation, the only one in that whole crazy krewe who maintained a home with kids and a garden – and a Kerouac bivouac under the backyard tree. And she remained a mother figure until the end to hundreds of fans who would email her, and she'd write every one back, offering her advice and years of wisdom to help with any problem anyone else had.

She maintained a routine for at least the last decade of her life, where she would do emails in the morning, read from a stack of books beside her bed all afternoon, and by 5:00 it was okay to have a glass of wine and watch the local and then national Beeb news, then quiz shows or nature documentaries in the evenings.

She also had shelves full of Beat movies that I went through and had us systematically watch every damn one, and I could ask her any question, and we'd hit pause and go off on crazy tangents and get another glass of wine and maybe watch another five minutes then something else would come up and it would take us about ten hours to get through one movie!

And she'd often say to whoever was talking in a documentary, "That isn't how it was!" and be correcting the history as it was being presented. The funniest time was when she was yelling at the screen, "That's completely wrong! You don't know what you're talking about!" *and it was her being interviewed!*

She is survived by her beloved son John Allen Cassady — named for Kerouac, Ginsberg and Neal — but

she called him Johnny. As well as by her daughter Jami
Cassady-Ratto, and her first-born Cathy Cassady-Sylvia,
as well as her grandchildren Jamie, Becky and Bill,
and her great-grandchildren Jon, Ellie, David, Bradley,
Elizabeth, Elliott and . . . Cody.

Carolyn rocked —
   but she also held down the Beat so others could solo.

Carolyn Cassady   1923 – 2013   R.I.P.

Part Three

Neal Cassady

and The Evermore

13

I Knew / Not Knew
Neal Namaste

I never met the Fastestmanalive
but I've gone coast-to-coast
with him and back

I never saw his blue eyes sparkle
but I saw his eyes
in friends who burned

I never had him read my mind
but I read his mind
in letters home

I never saw his skin grow gray
but I saw the grays
he colored bright

I never heard his manic voice
but heard him speak
in every jazz club "Go!"

I never took a joint he passed
but heard he was Bogie
before there was a Bogart

I never had him drive my car
but I learned his speed
with the windows down

I never saw him walk into a room
but he taught me
how to walk onto a stage

I never saw him make love to a woman
but I knew a woman
he loved for a life

I never saw him perform with the Dead
but I heard him through them
a thousand nights over

I never rode shotgun as he cut around corners
but I caught the trick
and mastered both seats

I never knew the man named Neal
but I never knew
a time I didn't.

14

Poem For Neal

by
George Walker

I went to walk the railroad, stepping with care along
Neal's last tracks.
They found him there, you know,
now 40 years ago.
Some say he'd breathed his last
When dawn's first rays revealed him to someone who
passed.
And there they ended, Neal's too few days.

Others said his heart held yet a few more beats,
When he was hauled unceremoniously through these streets
In some long forgotten pickup truck.
One thing was sure:
that night he'd run clear out of luck!

Then rumors flew and stories grew until it was clear
Nobody knew what happened here that cold dark fatal night,
When Cassady's spirit took it's final earthly flight.

Some spoke of cause and blame
Others said it was a shame
He'd left so soon.

The party hadn't ended yet.
Come, join the party! Place another bet!
But his chips were cashed,
And nobody knew just how he spent
Those last few cents.

Now, still, the questions fly:
Why here? How now? What potion's given, and by
whom?
Did some mislead him to his doom? From which house,
which room?
Were there words? A fight?
Did he just wander off that night?
Did he take a car, or walk? How far?

Some even claimed he counted ties,
Which just brings up more wheres and whys.
So I went and looked there by the tracks;
I didn't find him, of course.

Neal was long gone, past all guilt and remorse,
But the Beat goes on!

15

The Grateful Dead —
Jack Manifested As Music

Written: January 2017
Originally published in: Kerouac On Record,
    Bloomsbury Press, 2018

The Grateful Dead were Jack manifested as music.

Their essence was born of the road and adventures. They worked in improvisational music much like spontaneous prose. They broke every rule in showbiz … then broke every concert record there is — just as Kerouac broke every rule of grammar then had over 50 books in print.

Like Jack, the band had a prolific career whose output spanned multiple genres and decades, had many different co-conspirators, and found inspiration in the mythical characters of the West and the open Road. And they both considered Neal Cassady their driving force — in fact he literally drove each of them On The Road.

Both the Beats & the band had a core member who drank himself to an early grave, and others who spent considerable time & effort exploring the benefits of psychotropic drugs. Both groups were largely based out of San Francisco, and both had New York as their other home. And in fact it was the very same neighborhoods of both cities — North Beach and Greenwich Village — where each came of age before growing out into the rest of the city and world.

San Francisco has a centuries-old history of radicals, rebellion and reinvention. From Jack London to John Muir, Haight-Ashbury to Silicon Valley, the Bay Area has nurtured iconoclasts and outcasts, fostering new paradigms since its founding, be they environmental or cyber, free love or free jazz, gay rights or immigrant's plights. Hence, when Carolyn Robinson first moved to the city and planted the flag that would beckon her future husband Neal Cassady years before Lawrence Ferlinghetti or any other Beats ever set foot in the place, it was a town that already personified everything the burgeoning movement was about. It was an outsiders' oasis, a North American version of a European masterpiece of architecture to inspire every walking breath, a multi-hilled town of innumerable little villages, each with a thousand stories pouring out of every 3-story Victorian house.

And Jack fell in love — not only with Carolyn and his life-brother Neal — and so much so that he actually moved there briefly with his mother in 1957 — but also with the mirror city spirit of his beloved New York — the jazz clubs, the neighborhood bars, the openness and effervescent ever-changing characters and concepts that sprung from every 5-cent coffee or 10-cent beer. And just as the Beats' work brought this open-minded life-embracing sense of Adventure to the rest of the world, so too did the music that manifested there in the mid-'60s. Bob Dylan may have gone electric on the East Coast, but the real electricity of the kool-aid of cool rock came from the West, young man.

The Dead were proud flag-waving Beats who were keeping the beat in a whole new way. Just as Jack took a novel approach to novel construction, the band did the same with song structure. Just as Jack soloed on the keys stretching his flow and ideas to places heretofore unseen, so did that other J, Jerry, play his lines into a whole new space unheard in music save for the best of Jack's beloved Bebop. The Dead were not only the natural progression of the music of the Beats — but also of the very city that was home to both. In fact, Jack was so comfortable with each, he easily recast *The Subterraneans* events from New York to San Francisco in just three days of storytelling.

Unlike most bands and authors, both the Grateful Dead and Kerouac's popularity only grew after their primary heartbeat stopped — with the Dead's 2015 Fare Thee Well shows in Chicago breaking TicketMaster, pay-per-view, and Soldier Field all-time records — and Kerouac having roughly four times as many books in print today as he did the day he died. Not to mention the thousands of Dead-based bands playing around the world as you're reading this, or the hundreds of copies of *On The Road* that will be bought every day that you have this book in your hands.

Yet they both had inauspicious professional debuts (the Dead's eponymous first album and Jack's *The Town and The City*) — which in most cases would have presaged an undistinguished career — and certainly not be indicative of an artist who would end up changing their medium and worldwide culture.

And both had an unusually strong affinity for the other's form. Garcia was a voracious reader of books, and few novelists lived a life with as strong a connection to music as Jack. And the Grateful Dead were the only band that ol' Jack or Neal would ever sit in with.

Really it was — as it always seems to be — Neal Cassady at the center of the whole damn thing. No other rock band can claim anywhere near as close a connection to any one of the key Beats as the Grateful Dead can with their brother Neal. He lived at their house, ate at their table, drove their bus, performed on stage with them, and directly inspired some of their most oft-performed songs — including 'The Other One' and 'Cassidy.' Not to mention that 'Truckin'' is a musical *On The Road*, or 'Wharf Rat' is their *Big Sur*, or 'Attics of My Life' their *Book of Dreams*, or that 'Mexicali Blues' echoes *Mexico City Blues*, or 'China Cat Sunflower' could have been lifted from *Old Angel Midnight*, and on and on.

But Cassady . . . Cassady . . . Cassady . . . the guy Jack most wanted to impress, ditto Allen — the Mighty Muse — and just as with the Beats, he was there from the beginning with the Dead — on the bill or on the stage at many of the original Acid Tests including their now-legendary first big-venue gig — The Trips Festival — at the Longshoreman's Hall in S.F. in January '66.

On hanging with Neal, Jerry Garcia told *The History of Rock n Roll* documentarians, "Cassady was such an overwhelming ... *trip!* He was *so* singular. For one thing, he was *the* best sight-gag / physical comedy person. He had an incredible mind. He would do this thing, he did it to everybody — where you might not see him for months, and he would pick up *exactly* where he left off the last time he saw you. Like, *in the middle of a sentence!* First of all, you'd go, 'What the hell?' And then you'd realize, 'Oh yeah, this is that story he was telling me last time!' It was so mind-boggling, you couldn't believe he was doing it.

"He was also the first person I met who he himself was the art. He was an artist, and he was also the art. And he was doing it consciously. He worked with the world. His face could go through millions of expressions and contortions, and his body language was *so* communicative. It was *amazing*. He was like a musician in a way. ... It was an art form that hasn't been discovered yet ... something between philosophy and art.

"Off and on he stayed in our attic when we were at 710 [Ashbury St.]. He had a little camp up there with a mattress and his old chinos, and he'd come in and live

there for a week or so, every month or couple of months."
And it wasn't just Neal Cassady they housed. Furthur
on down The Road the band began to cover original Beat
Herbert Huncke's rent at the Chelsea Hotel until the day
he died.

And it wasn't just Neal and Huncke they were in
bed with, but right from the git-go, at that Trips Festival,
the group was sharing the bill with Allen Ginsberg and
Michael McClure, and the following January of '67, they
were the climactic band at the pivotal '60s birth day
party — the Human Be-In in Golden Gate Park — sharing
the stage with Allen, Michael, Gary Snyder, Lawrence
Ferlinghetti and Lenore Kandel.

But as much as they were born directly out of the
general Beat milieu, it was Jack and Neal specifically who
were their core influence. As Jerry told Al Aronowitz:
"After I read *On The Road*, I began to hear rumors
that it was about real people. When I heard that," and
Jerry broke into a grin, "I *had* to meet them." After
first meeting a few North Beach imposters who were
scamming their dinner off being 'the real Dean Moriarty'
he finally encountered the genuine article. Jerry went on:
"It was Neal who taught Kerouac how to write. Jack was
trying in very orthodox ways until Neal got him off of it.
Jack learned from Neal's manuscripts. I've read them.
He wrote like he talked. He could keep me spellbound for
hours. Nobody could tell a story like Neal. He had the
best timing. Someday his manuscripts'll all be published
and recognized."

In fact, it was going 'on the road' with the real

Moriarty a few years later that caused Garcia to make the commitment to the band instead of painting. As he told Babbs for he & Kesey's *Spit In The Ocean* special Neal issue, "Cassady did something that changed my life. It was after the Acid Test in Watts. I hit him up for a ride back to our house, and it was just me and him for some reason. He was mellow Neal, just a guy, just like us. But there was a mysterious thing there. I had a feeling that I was involved in a lesson.

"I was flashing on Neal as he was driving that he is one of these guys that has a solitary kind of existence, like the guy who built the Watts Towers, one person fulfilling a work. And I made a decision that night to be involved in something that wasn't a solitary pursuit. I was oscillating at the time. I'd originally been an art student and was wavering between one-man / one-work, or being involved in something that was dynamic and ongoing, and something in which you weren't the only contributing factor. That night I decided to go with what was dynamic and more than one mind was involved with. The decision I came to in the car with Neal was to be involved in a group thing — and I'm still involved in it."

Furthur, the very last question in the very last interview Garcia ever gave on camera (to the Silicon Valley Historical Association), was about Neal Cassady. "I got to be good friends with him. He was one of those guys that truly was a very *special* person. In my life, psychedelics and Neal Cassady are almost equal in terms of influence on me.

"Neal *was* his own art. He wasn't a *musician*, he

was a 'Neal Cassady.' He was a set of one. And he was it. He was the whole thing — top, bottom, beginning, end, everything. And people knew it. And people would be drawn to it. He was an unbelievable human being — the energy that he had, and the vocabulary he had of gestures and expressions — oh boy he was funny! Phew! I really loved him." ... were the last words Jerry Garcia ever spoke on camera.

The Dead's main lyricist, Robert Hunter, who actually met Cassady before Kesey did at a communal house nicknamed 'The Chateau' in Menlo Park not far from Kesey's Perry Lane scene in Palo Alto, said of Cassady to *Relix* magazine, "He was flying circles above me. He used to visit me a lot. He paid me the compliment of saying that when he goes to New York, he visits Bill Burroughs and when he comes here, he hangs at my house.

"He was Mr. Natural for us. He would say things and, if you had him on tape and could listen back, you could hear replies you hadn't heard before — multifaceted replies. The man was phenomenal, a phenomenal brain. Yeah, he was a *wonderful* guy.

"It was hard *not* to be Neal after he was around. He was such a master of any social situation that you'd learn it yourself, and when he was away it would take weeks before you'd stop being Neal. This was true of all of us. He was such ... an original. He had such a dynamic life and it was just *packed*. He just enjoyed the *hell* out of it."

Of the music in Jack's writing, Hunter said —

"That's bop!" And he later put his voice where his heart was and read from *Visions of Cody* as part of the *kicks joy darkness* CD, and was the voice of Dr. Sax on the audio recording of Jack's play *Doctor Sax and The Great World Snake.*

John Perry Barlow, the Dead's other lyricist, who wrote the words to *Cassidy* among many others, called Neal "The Most Amazing Man I Ever Met" (capitalization his). Bassist Phil Lesh phrased it, "Neal was the closest thing to poetry in motion I've ever seen." Garcia called him "the 100% communicator" and "the powerhouse of the Acid Tests." And those were gatherings with a lot of power! Imagine yourself at an evening with Neal Cassady, Allen Ginsberg, Ken Kesey, the Merry Pranksters, the Grateful Dead, and a barrelful of Owsley's freshest!

At one of those early Tests, rhythm guitarist and band youngster Bob Weir discovered that Ginsberg "was pretty damn amazing, the stuff he would say and do. So I figured, okay, I'm gonna sit next to this guy, which was okay with him."

To *Garcia* biographer Blair Jackson, Weir said, "When I fell in with Ken Kesey and Neal Cassady, it seemed like home sweet home to me, to be tossed in with a bunch of crazies. There was some real serious crazy stuff going on . . . For one thing, I had to abandon all my previous conceptions of space and time. ... I thought I was pretty well indoctrinated into the 'anything goes' way of life, but I found much more than anything goes with the Pranksters. There was a world of limitless possibilities. It was ... God, it's hard to say anything that doesn't sound clichéd, but it was really a whole new reality for this boy. We were dealing with stuff like telepathy on a daily basis.

"We picked up a lot from those guys. Particularly from Cassady. He was able to drive 50 miles-an-hour through downtown rush-hour traffic, he could see around corners — I don't know how to better describe it. And that's useful if you're playing improvisational music; you can build those skills to see around corners, 'cause there are plenty of corners that come up. We gleaned that kind of approach from Cassady. He was one of our teachers, as well as a playmate."

Another time Weir went even furthur — "We're all siblings, we're all underlings to this guy Neal Cassady. He had the guiding hand." Describing hanging with Neal, he said, "It was pretty freeform, but it was also — I hate to use the word cosmic, but I don't know how else to describe it. We were together in this big mind meld, and he would be having a conversation with what was going on in your head."

At their first show after hearing the news that Neal had died [Feb. 4th, 1968] — on Valentine's Day at the Carousel Ballroom in S.F. — Garcia made a special announcement, something he *never* did, and dedicated their show to Cassady.

As Phil put it in his Grate book *Searching For The Sound*, "I truly believe we were channeling Neal that night. The music was such a living thing: growing and changing from bar to bar, with his turn-on-a-dime responsiveness to context and novelty. When we listened back to the show, it was spectacular — vivid, protean, and relentless." In fact, right away they realized the Neal-channeled series of songs that flowed out that night should be the sequence for their upcoming studio/live amalgam album *Anthem Of The Sun* released later that year. And that's what they did, including with live tracks from this Neal show as part of it.

Phil devoted much ink in his memoir to this milestone moment in his life, including, "It hardly seemed credible that a life force like his, so generously endowed with the *rhythm* of motion through time, could be smothered and shut down at such an early age. ... Neal's death had hit me harder than I knew; I'd been obsessing on the loss of one of the most inspiring people I'd ever known personally. . . . . I vowed to myself that in the future I would live up to Neal's inspirational example." When Neal & Carolyn Cassady's only son John heard this passage read aloud he broke down at his palace and started crying.

"His life is nowhere near over," Weir told *On The Road* director Walter Salles decades after Neal's passing. "He lives in me and through me, especially when I'm on stage. He was more present than any human I've ever met. What I didn't learn I just osmoted from him. Living purely and completely in The Moment. What he saw in the present was an accumulation of all things past and future. 'Now' is all he was really involved with. That's what I've always drawn from when I'm playing — forget everything and just be there."

And speaking of forgetting everything — Weir often tells the miraculous story of how he wrote the last verse of 'The Other One' with the now-famous line — "The Bus came by and I got on, that's when it all began; There was Cowboy Neal at the wheel of the Bus to Nevereverland" — on the very day Neal was busy dying in Mexico. He furthur elaborates that at their first show back in S.F. (when Garcia made the stage announcement) they debuted the just-written Neal verse. Great story. Only problem is, pretty much every Dead show was recorded, and you can hear him singing that verse in every version for months before Neal died. Which, on the upside, means Neal coulda heard them sing it.

A much more reliable songwriting story is lyricist Barlow's account of the song *Cassidy* — in his essay 'Cassidy's Tale' — where he describes writing it about both Neal's death and the birth of a daughter within the Dead family named Cassidy. "This is a song about necessary dualities: dying & being born, men & women, speaking & being silent, devastation & growth, desolation & hope.

"I didn't actually meet Neal Cassady until 1967, by which time the Furthur bus was already rusticating behind Kesey's barn in Oregon, and the Grateful Dead had collectively beached itself in a magnificently broke-down Victorian palace at 710 Ashbury Street.

"Cassady was still very much Happening. Holding court in 710's tiny kitchen, he would carry on five different conversations at once and still devote one conversational channel to discourse with absent persons and another to such sound effects as disintegrating ring gears or exploding crania. To log into one of these conversations, despite their multiplicity, was like trying to take a sip from a fire hose.

"With a face out of a recruiting poster (leaving aside a certain glint in the eyes) and a torso, usually raw, by Michelangelo, he didn't even seem quite mortal. Though he would shortly demonstrate himself to be so.

"The front room of the second floor had once been a library and was now the location of a stereo and a huge collection of communally-abused records. He had set up camp on a pestilential brown couch in the middle of the room, at the end of which he kept a paper bag containing most of his worldly possessions.

"In the absence of other ears to perplex and dazzle, Neal went to the music room, covered his own with headphones, put on some Bebop, and became it, dancing and doodley-oooping a cappella to a track I couldn't hear. While so engaged, he juggled the 36 oz. machinist's hammer which had become his trademark. The articulated jerky of his upper body ran monsoons of sweat and the hammer became a lethal blur floating in the air before him."

The Dead's most obvious Kerouac-reflective song is their anthemic Road ode 'Truckin'.' Like Jack's roman à clefs, the song is autobiographical, and was literally written *on the road* by Hunter, with music by Jerry, Phil & Bob. And like Jack's *Road*, it largely defined their entire oeuvre to the general public. The song unabashedly celebrates Road life, Adventure, traveling, drugs, sleeplessness, getting into and out of trouble, and heading out to the streets just to see what you could find.

And just as Jack's *Road* line "the only people for me are the mad ones ..." became his most quoted, this Road song's phrase, "What a long strange trip it's been" became the Dead's, and has become so much a part of American vernacular it's been used by Congressmen on the floor of the House of Representatives, appeared in headlines on all manner of non-Dead-related stories and in book titles ranging from law to nature, and is even a level to achieve in some online video games like World of Warcraft (of all things)!

And speaking of lines that lasted — Bill Graham's quote that was ultimately painted onto the outside of Winterland — "They're not the best at what they do, they're the only ones that do what they do." — is their default epigram and seems to still get proven by the day.

Another line from 'Truckin'' worthy of Kerouac — "Chicago, New York, Detroit it's all on the same street" — is brought to life in part by the playful use of the preposition "on." Besides the wonderfully surreal psychedelic visual of cities weaving in and out on the same street — all blurring into one as you travel them — but also that they're all on the same road — as in "all roads lead to Rome." From most anywhere in North America, New York (and Adventure!) is on the street outside your front door — you just have to make a few turns to get there.

The song also has a reference to "soft machine" — quite possibly Burroughs's novel being name-checked. After all, as Weir revealed in a 1966 interview, they considered calling themselves Reality Sandwich at one point! (The Ginsberg book with that title came out on City Lights Books in 1963.) But this song — that never would have existed without the band members' mutual love of *On The Road* — was so resonant it never dropped out of their live repertoire from the time it debuted in August 1970 through their final shows with Garcia in July 1995.

As their drummer Bill Kreutzmann said in his book *Deal,* he'd read *On The Road* even before he'd met the rest of the band, and described how "It became influential to me in the same way that certain music was influential. It was jazz on the page ... it was a boarding pass out of Palo Alto and into destinations unknown — my life's great adventure. ... that there was something greater out there, and even if it didn't appear within my reach, I could grab ahold of it anyway, just by believing it was possible. That's really important. Because after that, I started reaching for it. And sure enough, I was able to grab ahold."

Or as their first co-manager Rock Scully sketched the band's North Beach birth in his memoir *Living with The Dead*: "The hungry i, Vesuvio's, and City Lights were our shrines. Kerouac, Kesey, Corso, Burroughs and Ginsberg were our holy madmen. We idolized the Beats ... Jerry was 15 when *On The Road* came out, and it became his bible ...."

And what would you say if I told you the most important poetry reading in Beat history was brought to you by the most important teacher in young Garcia's life?

It's true!

Wally Hedrick was the connecting rod. He was one of the six artists & poets who opened the Six Gallery on Fillmore Street in San Francisco in 1954. By the following summer, Wally had emerged as their event director, staging what years later would be known as "happenings" — poetry and music performances in the middle of an art gallery with a rainbow of participating creative people, many in an altered consciousness. By the summer of '55 he asked a young on-the-scenester Allen Ginsberg if he wanted to put on a reading there. According to Wally — Allen said no. Then he finished 'Howl.' Then he said yes.

```
              6 POETS AT 6 GALLERY

        Philip Lamantia reading mss. of late John
        Hoffman-- Mike McClure, Allen Ginsberg,
        Gary Snyder & Phil Whalen--all sharp new
        straightforward writing-- remarkable coll-
        ection of angels on one stage reading
        their poetry. No charge, small collection
        for wine and postcards. Charming event.

                 Kenneth Rexroth, M.C.

        8 PM Friday Night October 7,1955

           6 Gallery 3119 Fillmore St.
                    San Fran
```

Allen's typed postcard invitation.

On October 7th, 1955, with young Ginzy as
the catalyst and publicist, Wally and The Six put on
a 'charming event' (as Allen called it) — "Six Poets at
Six Gallery" — which became the coming-out party
for the Beats. What the Human Be-In and London's
International Poetry Incarnation were for the generation
a decade later, this was the moment the participants
all first realized there was a larger community of like-
minded souls than they thought. These were The Big
Three public events ... which were followed by Monterey
Pop, Woodstock, the US Festival, Live Aid and so on
... but these were the first magic mass moments that
spawned a cultural / consciousness revolution.

M.C.ed by the unofficial poet laureate of San
Francisco at the time, Kenneth Rexroth, it featured a
23-year-old Michael McClure in his very first poetry
reading (who also writes about the evening extensively

in his *Scratching The Beat Surface*); a couple of Philips, Whalen and Lamantia; a young nature lover named Gary Snyder raving on about 'A Berry Feast'; and one Allen Ginsberg reading' Howl' in public for the first time. "It drew a line in the sand," as McClure put it, for confessional, honest, candid, sexual, rebellious Beat poetry, and which prompted attendee Lawrence Ferlinghetti to send Allen a telegram the next day — "I greet you at the beginning of a great career. When do I get the manuscript?" refraining Ralph Waldo Emerson's famous letter to Walt Whitman upon experiencing *Leaves Of Grass*.

Kerouac himself was also present, but in the capacity of a "Go" yelling cheerleader and Go-for-wine running ringleader, gathering up change from "the rather stiff audience" and nipping out to score "three huge gallon jugs of California Burgundy and getting them all piffed," as he vividly described the night in his Northern California adventure novel, *The Dharma Bums,* where he also mentions how a reserved Neal Cassady and his girlfriend-of-the-moment Natalie Jackson (one month before her death) were also present at this historic evening that's widely and rightly regarded as the public Birth of the Beat Generation.

And wouldn't you know it, but Doctor Wally who delivered this baby became an art teacher at the California School of Fine Arts where a couple years later a wayward young artist named Jerry Garcia would enroll in what he described as the only school he was proud of attending. Hedrick became not only his teacher but a guiding force in Garcia's discovery of the Bohemian arts, at one point telling the young rebel who was still without applause that he and his friends were the real Beat Generation.

The historian Dennis McNally wrote such a Grate biography of Kerouac and the world around him, *Desolate Angel*, that Jerry anointed him to be the band's publicist and write the official history of the Grateful Dead, which he eventually did, called *A Long Strange Trip*. (There it is again!) In it he shares the detail of how Hedrick "... sent Garcia over to City Lights Bookstore to pick up Jack Kerouac's *On The Road*, a book that changed his life forever. Kerouac's hymn to the world as an explorational odyssey, an adventure outside conventional boundaries, would serve as the blueprint for the rest of Garcia's life."

Then there was Jack's "secret' skid row hotel' as he described S.F.'s Mars Hotel in *Big Sur* that the Dead would later immortalize as the title and cover of their 1974 studio album, and is seen (sadly) being demolished in *The Grateful Dead Movie*.

The way Garcia himself remembered his transformation — as captured in the liner notes for the 1990 Rhino re-release of Jack's three records put together by James Austin — "I recall in 1959 hanging out with a friend who had a Kerouac record, and I remember being impressed — I'd read his stuff, but I hadn't *heard* it, the cadences, the flow, the kind of endlessness of the prose, the way it just poured off the page. It was really stunning to me. His way of perceiving music — the way he wrote about music and America — and the road, the romance of the American highway, it struck me. It struck a primal chord. It felt familiar, something I wanted to join in. It wasn't a club, it was a way of seeing. It became so much a part of me that it's hard to measure; I can't separate who I am now from what I got from Kerouac. I don't know if I would ever have had the courage or the vision to do something outside with my life — or even suspected the possibilities existed — if it weren't for Kerouac opening those doors."

Or there was the time later in life when Jerry was looking back in a *Rolling Stone* interview and said, "I read *On The Road* and fell in love with it, the adventure, the romance of it, everything. I owe a lot of who I am and what I've been and what I've done to the Beats from the fifties. **I feel like I'm part of a continuous line of a certain thing in American culture, of a root … I can't imagine myself without that — it's what's been great about the human race and gives you a sense of how great you might get, how far you can reach.** And I think the rest of the guys in this band all share stuff like that. We all have those things, those pillars of greatness to lean on. If you're lucky, you find out about them, and if you're not lucky, you don't. And in this day and age in America, a lot of people aren't lucky, and they don't find out about these things."

Or there were the liner notes Robert Hunter wrote for the *One Fast Move Or I'm Gone* DVD where he said, "We have the scriptures of a butterfly dreaming he is a man dreaming himself a butterfly.

"Jack captured the guts of his own soul, if not the soul of our times, in torrential cloudbursts of exalted prose, egotistical letters, improbably immature journals — both drunken and sober — for all to see. And he did want us to see. Why? God knows ... but he did, and we have, and there you go. Maybe so that, despite all, we would love him. And we do. Case closed."

Another uncanny brotherly commonality between Jack & Jerry (besides both losing their fathers at a relatively young age) was how they both meticulously archived and preserved their own work. Whether due to an awareness of their legacy or simply for practical creative purposes, you're hard-pressed to find a writer who maintained better records or a band who recorded more performances. Jack regularly drew on his filing cabinets full of letters and notebooks to produce his next book, and the Dead would listen to how their alchemy sounded out in the room beyond the circle of players. And both these archives would turn out to be invaluable historically and financially as there were vaults of material that could be drawn on in the years after their passing.

And then there were the drugs.

Lots and lots of drugs. Miracle drugs. Drugs that could make you see through walls and time and space. Drugs no one outside small circles had even heard of. Drugs like yagé (aka ayahuasca) that Bill & Allen travelled to South America to experience, then wrote *The Yage Letters* about, or mescaline that Aldous Huxley did the same with in *The Doors of Perception*. And wouldn't you know it, but just as the young Warlocks were beginning to stir their cauldron, a great big Bear ambled out of the woods and poured in a bucket of LSD.

Both Kesey and Hunter participated in the government's early tests on the drug at the Veterans' Administration Hospital in Menlo Park circa 1959/60, and a young chemist on the scene named Augustus Owsley Stanley III, aka Bear, knew how to decipher formulas in science books and recreate them in his basement. Suddenly the mind-altering that Jack & Neal and all the Beats had gone out of their way (and into jail) in pursuit of was available in 3D rainbows on the corner for a dollar.

As Carolyn Cassady describes in her rivetingly real *Off The Road*, Jack & Neal first experimented with peyote (to not much effect) in 1952. Jack had another less-than-satisfactory experience on ether with the artist Jordan Belson in 1955, but a much more successful trip was taken on mescaline (the active ingredient in peyote) in October 1959, prompting Jack to write a 5,000-word 'Mescaline Report,' and tell Allen in a letter right afterward that he planned to take mescaline monthly "and am rarin to try lysurgic [sic] next" (after hearing Allen's recommendation following his first trip in May '59 — although Jack never followed through on either as far as we know). He also added, "... if everybody in the world took mescaline but once there would be eternal peace."

He wrote Allen again about the trip in June the next year, still raving, "When on mescaline I was so bloody high I saw that all our ideas about a 'beatific' new gang of worldpeople, and about instantaneous truth being the last truth, etc. etc. I saw them as all perfectly correct and prophesied, as never on drinking or sober I saw it — Like an angel looking aback on life sees that every moment fell right into place and each had flowery meaning."

Allen also mentioned that Jack took ayahuasca/ yagé in October 1960, and claims he said, "This is one of the most sublime or tender or lovely moments of all our lives together"; but in a later letter Jack referred to "visions of horror as bad as the Ayahuasca vision" so it seems he didn't process it as positively as Allen remembered him doing.

Jack also took psilocybin with Timothy Leary at Allen's apartment on East 2nd St. in January '61, and although he arrived already drunk and caused Leary to have "my first negative trip" (as he later confessed to Allen), but he described the experience quite favorably to Leary in a letter. "The faculty of remembering names and what one has learned, is heightened so fantastically that we could develop the greatest scholars and scientists in the world with this stuff ... There's no harm in Sacred Mushrooms if taken in moderation as a rule and much good will come of it." This was also the trip where Jack said the now widely quoted, **"Walking on water wasn't built in a day."**

He also wrote Allen about taking mushrooms one last time (in Dec. '61), and wanting to send a telegram to Winston Churchill, "thinking, on psilocybin, one baron to another, he'd understand." And although there's a photo of Jack by Allen taken in his 5th St. apartment in the fall of '64 captioned "a moment on D.M.T. visions," Kerouac ultimately concluded of tripping "I wrote nothing of value on it," and he never went back.

Where Jack & the Beats had come of creative age breaking open Benzedrine inhalers and scrambling to find leafy ditchweed, their younger brothers were handed a silver platter with a psychedelic splatter. It was the same pursuit of higher consciousness, but at a new '60s Space Age pace. Just as Jack was making leaps his father could never understand, so too did he have trouble keeping up with his offspring.

Starting before Jack left us and continuing decades afterwards, no single creative entity in America caused more people to go 'on the road' than did the Grateful Dead. They were Jack & Neal writ large. They were "The World's Largest Travel Agency" — both physically and psychically. Where Cassady expanded the Road trip from a Hudson to a school bus — the Dead turned the bus into a *Space*-ship.

They were the music of Jack's writing. There could be lulls and less-than-polished passages, but they were always leading to explosions of unequalled color and light and joy and life. And like Jack's books, the Dead's performances were not formulaic, conventional, predictable, or repetitious, and their songs celebrated the lives and aspirations of the American Everyman, the workingman — like one of their definitive albums,

Workingman's Dead. They both painted American
Beauty, lived on the American Road, sang songs of The
Road like Whitman before them, and spawned a trip that
more adventurers jumped on than any other in history.
Jack may have written the book, but the Dead extended
his vision into a functioning Road lifestyle that then
birthed a festival culture that is the thriving nationwide
Six Gallery of the 21st century.

 And the band put their money where their heart
was — including being primary funders of the On The
Road Jack Kerouac Conference in Boulder in 1982 (that
I wrote a whole firsthand Adventure Book about, *The
Hitchhiker's Guide to Jack Kerouac.*) That summit
— which included Ken Kesey and fellow core Merry
Pranksters Ken Babbs & George Walker, plus Abbie
Hoffman, Timothy Leary, and every living Beat from
Allen to Gregory to Bill to Holmes, along with all the key
women from Carolyn Cassady to Edie Kerouac to Jack's
daughter Jan, not to mention three shows by the band at
nearby Red Rocks Amphitheatre — ended up changing
the world's perception of Kerouac which had plummeted
to near irrelevancy in the 1970s. But that genius of
organization and promotion — Allen Ginsberg — in his
wisdom, brought together the '60s offspring, as well as all
the living original Beats, to rally the troops and share love
stories with the next generation of scholars, journalists,
academics, acolytes, practitioners & pranksters. The
result was an author who had been largely out-of-print
and out-of-mind began a resurgence that has continued
unabated to this day — all stemming from an event

funded by the Grateful Dead.

And that commitment didn't end with Garcia's passing in 1995 and the retirement of the Grateful Dead entity. *Kicks joy darkness* with Robert Hunter was 1997, his Dr. Sax portrayal in 2003, and the *One Fast Move Or I'm Gone* documentary was 2009. Phil Lesh's tribute to Neal came out in 2005, and Kreutzmann's reverential remembrance was 2015. In 2007, Bob Weir did a Kerouac-themed show in Jack's birthplace of Lowell, as well as a talk and Q&A with Jack and Dead biographer Dennis McNally. And both Weir & McNally gave extensive filmed interviews to Walter Salles in 2010 for a documentary about *On The Road* that has yet to be released.

They're still on about it to this day.

Love for real not fade away.

16

Floating Universities: The Power of The Collective in Art

In 1998 when I was helping the great and soulful Holly George-Warren put together The Rolling Stone Book of The Beats, *she said I could write about whatever angle I wanted. Twice. One subject I thought had never been properly explored (and still hasn't, really) is the power of the collective. Walter Salles & I touched on it in that earlier chapter here, but it's something that could still be explored a lot more. It's why we talk about a Beat "generation" and not one or two writers. The famous John Cohen photo on the cover of the* Rolling Stone *book features a novelist, a painter, a jazz & classical musician and a couple poets gathered together to make a film. The collective. Where the "we" is always bigger than the "me" and more colors on the palette make for the richer picture.*

Written: July–August 1998

Originally published in: The Rolling Stone Book of The Beats, *Rolling Stone Press, 1999*

Brian Hassett

Give me your befuddled masses,

Your rejection slips, pink slips, verbal slips, all;

Knock down the gates, throw open the bars,

The artists are having a ball.

Teach me, show me, let me in;

Challenge me, push me, help me win.

Athletes have their team

And suits can wear the firm,

But making art keeps you home alone,

And the tavern's the place you turn.

Solo suffering totally blows,

So into the sea you dive,

Searching for soles who swim like you

And act at least vaguely alive;

With deep sea wails you plunge the depths,

With freshwater poets you school,

With coral reefers you spark the sea,

Drinking in dreams from the pool.

Out of the one grow many, and out of many grows the One. The "It." The Ahhh. The Unspoken Thing. And from this desire for oneness, togetherness, the whole, artists from the Beat poets of the fifties to the women songwriters of Lilith have collaborated, cajoled and consoled each other into movements and generations.

"The Beat Generation" may never have had a single unified voice any more than Generation X does, but their range of harmonies ended up blending into a pretty inspiring choir.

The term was coined by Jack Kerouac, expounded upon by John Clellon Holmes in the *New York Times Sunday Magazine*, and endlessly championed by Allen Ginsberg, partly because the prior "generation" of disaffected visionary American writers had come up with the convenient "Lost Generation," thanks to Mama Stein. Hemingway — another pretty shrewd self-promoter — dropped her phrase as an epigraph to his first novel, *The Sun Also Rises*, and suddenly F. Scott Fitzgerald, Hart Crane, John Dos Passos, e.e. cummings et al were no longer a bunch of struggling writers, but a *generation*. "Yeah, that's it, we're a generation. Yeah." We're talkin' 'bout my g-g-generation. Suddenly lone authors joined a *team*, and instead of remaining disparate spindly voices drowned out by a raging torrent of daily fads and fixations, each of their challenging visions became buoyed by the others.

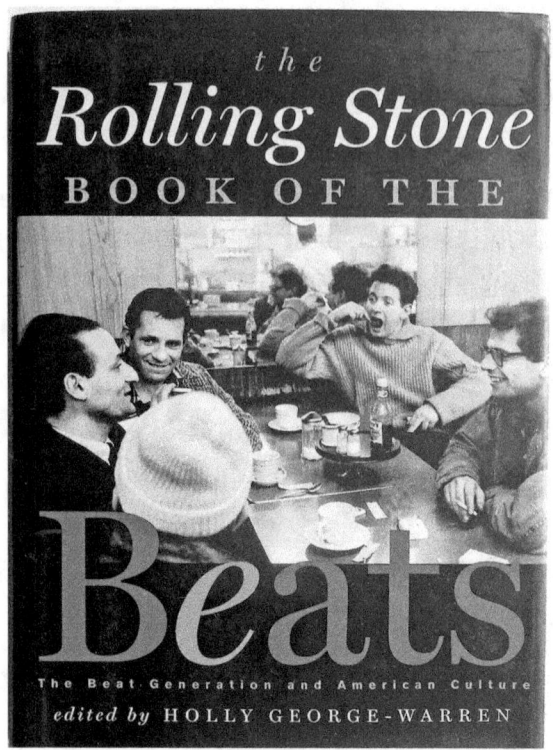

And in this supportive spirit a loosely defined Beat community became a very interdisciplinary affair as they freely mingled and collaborated with Abstract Expressionist painters, jazz musicians, Living Theater actors, playwrights, photographers, cartoonists, dancers, mystics and poets from other New York Schools. In smokin' Greenwich Village joints like the Cedar Tavern, the San Remo, and the Artists Club, something more than ideas were being exchanged.

"We were sharing the holy light," said composer David Amram, Kerouac's principal musical collaborator and the jazz laureate of the Generation. "The Artist's Club was a beautiful get-together run by artists for artists, with talking, philosophy, arguments and discussions by the hour by serious and brilliant people. Then afterwards we'd all go over to the Cedar Tavern and continue the rap. It was like a floating university."

The Cedar Tavern, now woven vibrantly into the quilt of New York City history, was the collective comfort zone for Jackson Pollock, Willem de Kooning, Franz Kline, Larry Rivers, Frank O'Hara, various art critics, and the Beats as they emerged on the scene. Located originally on 8th Street & University Place, it was a tiny tavern with no jukebox or anything else, deep in the heart of the Village when it still was one.

"We had a lot of love and a gigantic extended family of friends," Amram says of the Cedar scene. "You could sit at any table and hear the most inspiring conversations about art, theater, music, baseball, everyday living. It was an oasis, a mecca.

"There was a communal sense; we all helped each other rejoice in the struggle, rather than despairing, by always encouraging and paying attention to each other and trying to give that love and respect and interest, and also honest opinions and criticisms."

Nowhere is this collaborative spirit more visually animated than in the 1959 film *Pull My Daisy*, the single most illuminating Beat collaboration. Narrated by Kerouac's best 28 minutes on tape, captured in early cinéma vérité by evocative still photographer Robert Frank, playfully scored by the classically trained Amram who also appears as the friendly French hornist Mezz McGillicuddy, and starring Ginsberg, Gregory Corso and

Peter Orlovsky as themselves, this Lower East Side home movie is the only existing footage of the Beats in their prime other than a few scattered TV clips. Co-produced by painter Alfred Leslie and shot in his canvas-filled loft, featuring painter Larry Rivers in the role of Neal Cassady (who was sadly imprisoned in San Quentin for two joints of marijuana at the time), with art dealer Richard Bellamy as the bishop antagonist, and financed by Wall Street libertine painter Walter Gutman, it's a film made by painters about poets narrated by a novelist.

Another inspired collective on the path were the writers and artists of the Black Mountain College of North Carolina, an experimental Appalachian art school whose faculty included poets Charles Olson, Robert Creeley and Robert Duncan. Flourishing between 1950 and 1957 (when the school went bankrupt), their manifesto was Olson's 1950 essay "Projected Verse" which emphasized the transferral of energy between a poem's creator and reader. Their influential *Black Mountain Review* was one of the first regularly published collections of the wide-ranging free-verse voices of the new American poetry movement, with Creeley, William Carlos Williams and Denise Levertov appearing alongside Ginsberg, Kerouac and Gary Snyder. In 1952 the Black Mountaineers produced *Theater Piece 1*, America's first "happening" which teamed Olson's unfettered poetry with the work of artist Robert Rauschenberg, avant-garde musician John Cage and choreographer Merce Cunningham.

Also dancing in the klieg lights of collective freedom was the Living Theater, the iconoclastic company founded by Julian Beck and Judith Malina, who began their playful, interdisciplinary association in Greenwich Village in the late forties. In their first years of production (1951-1952), they staged plays by such diverse contemporary artists as Pablo Picasso, T.S. Eliot, Gertrude Stein, Kenneth Rexroth and John Ashbery. Rather than acting within the confines of conventional theater, they practiced street theater, confrontational theater, interactive theater, wholly *living* theater. As longtime member Steve Ben Israel described their method: "When you're an actor, you're waiting for a playwright to get an idea, or a director to do a play, or a producer to produce a play. And here we were, actors *creating* all of that — producing, directing, writing and acting it together with *our* specific message."

This same blessing of community has been felt by artists ranging from the High Renaissance in Florence to the also fairly high Poetry Renaissance in San Francisco. Most of the resident groundbreaking geniuses of Florence circa 1500 belonged to some regimented guild or patron's stable, so many of the artists like Michelangelo, Leonardo, Filippo Lippi and Rustici, along with architects, storytellers and poets, would also gather in their own mock confraternities.

In one of the more wacky images in art history, picture several of these blazing masters meeting as the Company of the Cauldron for lively drunken dinners around a giant cooking pot in one of their sculpture studios where they'd begin creating murals not with paint but with the chicken legs, sausages, cheese and jelly.

Even though their quarrels were nearly as colorful as their art, never has a generation of artists advanced their media so quickly. "Hi! I'd like you to meet my friend, *David*."

In San Francisco in the 1950s a community of poets began a similarly inspired coffeehouse collective, meeting and reading in the nooks and bookstores of North Beach. Embracing the Platonic adage, "To good men's parties good men flock unasked," the cultural outlaws from around the nation who'd gathered in this traditionally liberal port city were starting to notice the same faces on the same stages night after night. Poets like Gary Snyder, Michael McClure, Lawrence Ferlinghetti, Robert Duncan, Kenneths Patchen and Rexroth, assemblage artists like Bruce Conner and Wallace Berman, and filmmakers like Kenneth Anger and Harry Smith all began an enthusiastic crossover of interdisciplinary collaboration that was breaking society's birdbrained habit of pigeonholing artists. A lush flower garden had burst into bloom and it wasn't long before the psychedelic paisley ran wild.

In a sunshower of Day-Glo paint, Ken Kesey and his Merry Pranksters had a great notion to take the collective to an even higher level. Incubating in pools of acid on the edge of Stanford University, Kesey was forming an ever-expanding coterie of authors, intellectuals, artists & musicians that would eventually encompass Neal Cassady, the Grateful Dead and cherry Kool-Aid. As Intrepid Traveler Ken Babbs put it, "The Pranksters are a collective of that American spirit that's been passed on from the founding fathers through Melville, transcendentalism, Whitman, Faulkner, the Beats and *zoom* into the Pranksters where it took a wild turn of spontaneity in tribal dance, uninhibited jazz, nonsensical word raps and any other unfettered reaching of the spirit toward newfound freedoms."

A healthy dose of this Prankster ethic came from the pranksterish Dadaists who were trying to overthrow not only the rigidity of the fine arts in the 1910s and '20s, but civilization itself. By staging pranks in public places like cathedrals in the middle of a service, this gang of offbeat artists and authors had a collective effect on history rather than simply getting arrested as solo psychos.

And out of their inspired playfulness grew the more serious subconscious exploration of the Surrealists. Founded by the psychologist and poet André Breton, and including Salvador Dali, Joan Miró and René Magritte, the Surrealists strove to fuse our dreamscapes with reality, creating "an absolute reality, a surreality." Blending psychology, poetry and painting into a collage of the subconscious, the Surrealists were on a dedicated search for the meaning of life in the mysteries of the mind that Freud had only recently begun to unveil. Their direct channeling of the subconscious through trance-like states and automatic writing appealed to many artists of the time. Painter, occasional William Burroughs collaborator and regular cut-up Brion Gysin joined the Surrealists in Paris, as did future Beat poet Philip Lamantia in New York, who also helped edit their magazine *View*. But joining this group had a disturbing caveat: Namely, you could actually get expelled from it by Breton — as both Dali and Gysin were — for hanging with the wrong people or changing your mind, which is a curious condition for a mind-opening movement.

But along the way, the group had a lot of fun poking a carrot in the eye of the snobby Parisian art world as they painted green apples on faces and eyes in the middle of baked hams. Now picture Monty Python's cartoons of a head popping out of a foot, or scenes of a naked man playing an organ in a field. The Surrealists expanded on the illogical juxtaposition of thought earlier espoused by the French poets Apollinaire and Lautréamont and the line of their legacy is still being doodled.

And that's the great thing: As much as these cool collectives were happening in the recent past, many are thriving today. From communal artists' hearths like New York's Nuyorican Poets Cafe and Knitting Factory to attention-getting rock fests like Lilith Fair and the Tibetan Freedom Concerts, groups of like-minded people are still working together for the collective better.

"It's good for the soul, for one thing," Sheryl Crow said of joining the Lilith tour. "I mean, it's what religion's based on — that commune, the community, the solace and the fellowship of people who have a kindred spirit."

Whether it's painting the walls with dinner in Florence or breakfast in bed for 400,000 at Woodstock, coming together stretches the horizon beyond the sun of its parts. And you don't have to be half-a-million strong.

As George Harrison put it of his much smaller group, "That was the good thing about being four together. Not like Elvis, you know. I always felt sorry for him later 'cause he was on his own. He had his guys with him, but there was only one Elvis and nobody else knew what he felt like. But for us, we all shared the experience."

Being together counts. Even a collective of two. Supporting someone who is supporting you is the seed of a generation.

17

Abstract Expression: From Bird to Brando

The other subject I chose for The Rolling Stone Book of The Beats *and could also be expanded into a whole book is about that fascinating revolutionary decade at the center of the last century — 1945 to 1955.*

Written: June–July 1998
Published in: The Rolling Stone Book of The Beats,
        Rolling Stone Press, 1999

Fire lights and smoking nights
And splashes of dripping paint;
Jazz explosions and constant commotions
Leave It To Beaver this ain't.

It was the halftime show of the century!
        1945 to 1955.
        "We're gonna rock the rock in the second half."
        Or we're all gonna die.

Life was pretty uncertain after two world wars and two atomic bombs in too little time. By 1945, it could go either way and everybody knew it. Edward R. Murrow was on the wireless delivering graphic nightly accounts of the bombing of Europe. Centuries-old nations were tumbling by the month. Blackouts, rationing and depression were a way of life. The end was surely near. But leaning forward into this tension wind were some courageous artists transforming their media into gloriously honest expressions of the furthest and sometimes most beautiful reaches of our mind.

Through a door opened by Freud and into a room lit by Jung, Reich, Stanislavski, Breton and others, the expression of the subconscious self, the center, the soul, the truth, became the new goal of artists all over the world, some who happened to be drinking together, and others who were drinking alone.

During the same years that Jack was blowing apart the novel and Allen the poem, Jackson Pollock was exploding canvases on Long Island, Charlie Parker was breaking the sound barrier on 52nd Street, and Marlon Brando was ripping his chest open on Broadway. In nextdoor Midtown, it was television's "Golden Age" with *Your Show of Shows* inventing live sketch comedy, and *Kraft Television Theater* live weekly drama. Surfing the last of the vanishing vaudeville nightspots, Lord Buckley and Lenny Bruce were cutting their teeth before cutting the edge of stand-up comedy. And several new publications began appearing, from the *Village Voice* to

Playboy, bringing the edge to the middle of the country. In 1945, Jackson Pollock moved away from the nightly Village bar scene — with Franz Kline, Willem de Kooning, Frank O'Hara and roomfuls of other boozehounds — and out to the seclusion of a farmhouse in Springs, Long Island, to begin his dripping live action paintings. Where he came up with the idea is anybody's guess since the tormented alcoholic abstractionist was notoriously uncommunicative about his process. His sculptor-friend Constantine Nivola could at least explain the lead-up: "It was the Surrealists, such as Breton, who had the idea of releasing the tension in painting without any preconceived notions, letting the spontaneity do the actual painting." Pollock just took the idea to outer space. Or inner space. If you stand in front of one of his dripping paintings and stare into it for a while you can take a long strange trip without ever leaving the gallery. Somehow in the subconscious rhythms of Pollock's trance dance he created a mirror of our mind, patterns out of chaos, and motion out of stillness.

"It was great drama," filmmaker Hans Namuth said of watching him work. "The flame of explosion when the paint hit the canvas; the dancelike movement; the eyes tormented before knowing where to strike next; the tension; then the explosion again."

"When I am *in* my painting, I am not aware of what I'm doing," Pollock once said. When another brilliant Abstract Expressionist Hans Hofmann asked him about the use of nature in his work, he answered, "I am nature."

It was this firm belief in the natural flow of self that was propelling so many of these daring young artists in their flying seat pants. And remember — this was when gray was the national color, vanilla the flavor, conformity the goal, and McCarthyism the disease of the era. The slightest deviation in hair length or hemline meant you were a communist to many in this newly military-trained generation.

In November 1945, the same month that Pollock moved into the barn on Long Island, Charlie Parker moved into the WOR Studios in Midtown Manhattan to lay down some abstract expression of his own in what Savoy Records not unjustly called, "The greatest recording session in modern jazz." The first session ever under Parker's own name featured a little combo including Dizzy Gillespie and Miles Davis on trumpets and Max Roach on drums.

What Monk, Parker, Dizz, Miles and others had been working on the last few years of Monday night jam sessions at Minton's Playhouse in Harlem and the clubs along 52nd Street was the first big break in jazz since Louis Armstrong stretched the solo in his Hot Five and Hot Seven sessions in 1926. By improvising a new melody line based on the existing chords of 32-bar popular songs like "I've Got Rhythm," "Sweet Georgia Brown," and "How High The Moon," and often playing at double the tempo of the rhythm section, these bop-blazers created an unprecedented "skidilibee-la-bee you, —oo, —e bop she-bam," as Doctor Kerouac so accurately diagnosed it in "The Beginning of Bop."

Considered "almost telepathic" even by reserved jazz journals, Bird's frenetic speed carried him into the unknown every night, relying on the same subconscious instinctual current that Pollock was channeling. And this complete commitment to intuition was about to revolutionize American theater.

Get this: When Chekhov's first play *The Seagull* had its original production, it bombed so badly he vowed to never write another play. Then a young director named Konstantin Stanislavski came along with some wacky new idea about actors improvising from their own experience to fully convey the psychology of the characters, and he begs Chekhov for the rights to re-stage the play. This pivotal production heralds the birth of both the Moscow Art Theater and the Stanislavski "Method," and gives the playwright Anton Chekhov the encouragement to go on and write a few more plays you may have heard of.

Flip ahead to December 1947, New York City, and *A Streetcar Named Desire* with Marlon Brando is opening on Broadway. *This* pivotal production by Elia Kazan heralds the birth of both the Actors Studio and the Method in American theater, and gives the playwright Tennessee Williams the encouragement to go on and write a few more plays you may have heard of.

Stella Adler described *Streetcar's* lead and Greenwich Village resident Brando as "the perfect marriage of intuition and intelligence," but she could have been talking about any of these ice-breakers of the American art-ic.

Stanislavski's tenet was: "You must live the part every moment you are playing it." Like Bird, Jackson and Jack. Rather than perfect diction or posture, actors were encouraged to channel the center of their soul. The frame of dialogue was only a canvas to fill in from the actor's own experience.

And this same self-reliant philosophy was taking hold all over New York City. In 1950, with network television barely five years old, Sid Caesar and a few friends came up with this wild idea to do a funny 90-minute skit-driven show on Saturday night *live* on NBC. For the next four years, televised sketch comedy was being pioneered on *Your Show of Shows*, with writers like Woody Allen, Neil Simon and Mel Brooks first getting their pens wet.

That same year, Lord Buckley, the wailinest Beat comedian there ever was, was getting ready to hit the road after five years of developing his improvisational hipster style in New York's dives and dying vaudeville halls. Telling stories in his hipsemantic rap he'd "recast incidents from history and mythology into a patois that blended scat-singing, black jive, and the King's English," as biographer Oliver Trager summed it.

"Lord Buckley's a secret thing you pass under the table," Ken Kesey once explained of Buckley's lack of name recognition, even though his influence ranges from George Carlin to Jerry Garcia.

"Lord Buckley and Grateful Dead philosophy merge in a certain irony of viewpoint," Garcia told Trager. "The way he did his show was very dramatic. It would start off like a regular stand-up routine, but . . . it really turned into kind of a primal experience. A very powerful style with a lot of magic. You can't act it. You have to think of yourself *as* 'Lord Buckley.'"

In December of the same year (1950) Kerouac received "The Letter" — Neal Cassady's famous 16,000-word Joan Anderson/Cherry Mary epic (the known surviving portion brought jazzily to the screen in 1997 as *The Last Time I Committed Suicide*) — which would change Jack's approach to writing. "I have renounced fiction and fear," he wrote Cassady right back. "There is nothing to do but write the truth." And within a few months he'd finished *On The Road* in a single twenty-day stretch on a single roll of tracing paper in a single paragraph.

To best describe where his technique was coming from, Jack honored his friend Allen's request to write his "Essentials of Spontaneous Prose" and "Belief & Technique For Modern Prose":

> "Time being of the essence in the
> purity of speech, sketching language
> is undisturbed flow from the mind of
> personal secret idea-words, *blowing* (as
> per jazz musician) on subject of image.
> . . . Begin not from preconceived idea of
> what to say about image but from jewel
> center of interest in subject of image at
> *moment* of writing, and write outwards
> swimming in sea of language to peripheral

release and exhaustion. . . . Write 'without
consciousness' in semi-trance (as Yeats'
later 'trance writing'). . . . Struggle to
sketch the flow that already exists intact in
mind. Don't think of words when you stop
but see picture better."

And speaking of seeing better — that same year the
revered *Brave New World* author, Aldous Huxley, first
took mescaline and wrote a vivid and valuable account of
it in *The Doors of Perception*. Louis Armstrong was an
old teahead of time, Bird a heroin addict, Jack, Jackson
and Tennessee hard liquor drinkers, but this was a
whole new trip. Huxley's detailed and "inexpressibly
wonderful" account of exploring the amplified mind
opened The Doors for the psychedelic revolution that was
shimmering just around a corner on Haight Street.

In 1953 yet another scholarly study appeared that
would spark an even better revolution — Alfred Kinsey's
Sexual Behavior in the Human Female — whispering
in science that a quarter of all married women had
extramarital affairs and most women had multiple
premarital partners. (!) Ozzie was aghast and Harriet
blushed, but the secret was out. Sex *was* happening. As
part of his research, Kinsey even met with Tennessee
Williams, went to see *Streetcar*, and studied the actors'
sexual backgrounds. He also interviewed the Beats'
number one hustler Herbert Huncke, and in fact used
him to round up subjects. Too bad Cassady lived in San
Francisco.

In 1954, a nineteen-year-old Elvis Presley passed
through the doors of Sun Studios, and the whole world
snuck in behind him. Brando won the Oscar for *On The
Waterfront* the same year he was appearing all over the
country as the leather-clad leader of a motorcycle gang
called The Beetles in *The Wild One*. The possibilities of
what was commercially acceptable were changing forever.

By '55 the rockets of the renaissance began going
off like fireworks: James Dean's disaffected hipster goes
drag-racing with trouble *Rebel Without A Cause*; Rod
Serling's "Patterns" wins an Emmy as he begins tweaking
the summit of our imagination; the *Village Voice* and a
new journalism appears; Chuck Berry goes cruisin' with
Maybellene; Little Richard lets everybody know he's
Tutti Frutti all rootti — and *Billboard* begins tracking
its first "Pop" chart; Marilyn's white dress goes whoosh
in *The Seven Year Itch,* and the first birth-control pills
start working; Jack writes *Mexico City Blues* in a month,
giving it the inscription, "I want to be considered a jazz
poet blowing a long blues in an afternoon jam session on
Sunday;" Burroughs starts nibbling on his *Naked Lunch*,
Ferlinghetti snaps a few *Pictures of The Gone World*,
Ginsberg begins to *Howl* at the Six Gallery reading; and
the *On The Road* fame train is still two years away.

From Pollock's swirling strokes to splashing
color screensavers, from Brando reaching New York
audiences with *A Streetcar Named Desire* to Bravo
reaching nationwide living rooms with *Inside The Actors
Studio*, from Jack's punctuation-liberated prose to the

abbreviated brevity of online language, from Ginsberg freely howling to Richie Havens howling *Freedom*, the commitment to spontaneous subconscious expression of this pivotal mid-century decade intuited our new millennial lives in ways still being improvised.

Tom Wolfe Tribute

Event: Tom Wolfe's passing
Date: May 14th, 2018
Written: June 13th, 2018

We've had a flood of famous & important people dying the last few years. 2016 was the recent one most think of as the mass kill-off year that had us all praying for it to end — which it did, sadly, in November, with democracy and decency being cremated before our eyes.

The last famous person's death that really threw me — well, it was two in 2014 — Philip Seymour Hoffman and Robin Williams, both completely unexpected, and both inspirational teachers in my life.

But Tom Wolfe's passing on May 14th 2018 brought me to unexpected tears several times that day. And it was really because of one work — *The Electric Kool-Aid Acid Test.*

That book changed my life as much or more than any other. When I first read it at age 15 it blew open what was possible to this comfortable kid in Mayberry, Manitoba. Acid Tests . . . the Grateful Dead . . . road trips in a bus . . . a new way of talking . . . a new way thinking . . . a new way of *being*. A Prankster! Playful & goofing, but productive & curious. These weren't people sitting around waiting to be entertained — everything about them was proactive, and *doing*, and making things happen. And being funny! I wanted to be one of them — and I *became* one of them by my own actions, in consort with others. That book changed my approach on how to live, how to interact with others, how to be part of a collective, and I carried it with me into high-end concert production & low-level club shows, into life in a giant corporation & life within a tiny community.

As the years rolled on, I read a lot of other books — including Kerouac, who Wolfe in part hipped me to by writing about this Neal Cassady guy on the bus — and I began writing more and more seriously as the years went on. I was influenced by Dr. Seuss and William Shakespeare; James Joyce and Hunter Thompson; Dave Barry and Eugene O'Neill; the Beats and the rock poets. But as my writing and life evolved, I read less of the playwrights of my formative 20s, only occasionally dipped back into Dr. Seuss's playful mastery, and retained the lessons of Joyce without rereading him too often. But the one prose canvas, more than *On The Road* or *Huckleberry Finn* or *Fear & Loathing* that I kept returning to with jaw-dropped awe was *Electric Kool-Aid*

Acid Test.

As Kerouac wrote in a piece for *Writer's Digest* titled "Are Writers Made or Born?" — "It ain't whatcha write, it's the way atcha write it." And Tom Wolfe applied that playfulness to his playful subject, so perfectly reflecting in prose the scatological waves the Pranksters thought and operated. It's the greatest, most effective long-form blend of prose and subject I've ever come across.

Kesey said to me in a "you gotta hand it to the guy" way, and also thankfully put it on the record in a 1989 interview with NPR — "Wolfe's a genius. He did a lot of that stuff, he was only around three weeks. He picked up that amount of dialogue and verisimilitude without a tape recorder, without taking notes to any extent. He just watches very carefully and remembers."

Looking back on the oeuvres of literary masters of the 20th century, Wolfe joined a pretty esteemed group that included Jack Kerouac, John Clellon Holmes, Allen Ginsberg and Ken Kesey who wrote about that singular inspiration Neal Cassady — "smiling and rolling his shoulders this way and that and jerking his hands out to this side and the other side as if there's a different drummer somewhere, different drummer, you understand .... "

When I was writing *The Hitchhiker's Guide to Jack Kerouac,* every night that I went to bed still having the mind strength to read, it was *Electric Kool-Aid* that I'd open the pages of. Not *On The Road* or *Fear & Loathing*, but rather the guy who stretched language even Furthur, who left me in awe with the rules he would break paragraph after paragraph, while still maintaining a clear, gripping, fact-rich narrative. He was moving James Joyce up to the 1960s; he was breaking more rules than *The Subterraneans*; he was simultaneously being Pollock and Rembrandt.

Some people over the decades disparaged Wolfe, and *Electric Kool-Aid* in particular, and I think that caused me to not speak up for the book as much as I should have. But when he died, I realized how that one work changed my life. *Twice.* First in its subject matter . . . and years later in the mastery of its prose. And what brought me to tears was that I never told him that. Or anyone, really. I've met and spent time with most of the authors I admired who were alive when I was. Except Wolfe — even though we lived in the same city for a quarter century.

I regret not thanking him for changing my life. I regret not defending his writing. I regret not standing up for him, and not celebrating his book. I regret letting other people silence me, or make me think I must be wrong in my take on that book.

With Wolfe's passing, and my uncontrollable tears that day, I learned the tough lesson to never again be silenced by anyone else's opinion of a work of art — especially writing!

I need to get in touch with Kinky Friedman and Aaron Sorkin and Matt Taibbi before its too late!

Love your inspirations. And don't let anybody tell you otherwise. And if you can tell the creators while they're still alive — do it. Thoughts & prayers & platitudes aren't going to cut it for you or them after it's too late.

Acknowledgments and Gratitude

As Ken Kesey put it of how someone becomes a Merry
　　Prankster — "We just recognize each other."

I'd like thank the late great Carolyn Cassady for
recognizing me as a kindred spirit. We shared many of
the same qualities and traits and passions and interests,
and it led us to having an engaging surrogate mother-son
relationship — even though she already had the closest
one possible with her own pride & joy.

　　And speaking of that pride, one John Allen
Cassady, I'd like to thank for the same things, and sharing
his warped dry ever-present sense of humor, his easy
laugh, and his quest for Adventure — even when a little
bird on his shoulder may have chirped to hold back, he
kept going Furthur.

And while we're at it, I wanna thank his son Jamie & his wife Michelle for all they've been doing these last few years, and sisters Cathy & Jami for keeping the voices alive.

And I'd like to thank Sky for giving me the daily and weekly hours of space to paint this canvas, and for the inspiration and motivation to quit smoking cigarettes (on July 9th, 2018). And I'm also ever-Grateful to the mighty Jeff Mease who leant me Alan Carr's stop smoking CDs that did the trick. And to the Lucky Dawgz and their Bear's Picnic for giving me the goal line aspiration of a victory tent to celebrate.

And hugely to my L.A. brother S.A. Griffin for not only the wonderful riffing expansive introduction, but also being my DNA in Southern C.A. When Kesey was leaving the S.F. police station in January '66 after his second pot bust, he quoted to a television reporter a line from *Sometimes A Great Notion* — "I feel that a man has the right to be as big as he feels it in him to be." To my experience, S.A. Griffin has lived that admonition as well as anyone I've ever met.

And speaking of Kesey and the West Coast, I'd also like to thank my sometimes show partner George Walker for being a true brother of the stage, and for sharing his loving poem written in the ghost steps of Neal.

And to my Canadian compadre Dale "Gubba" Topham for being a crucial early reader and sounding board when the images were just coming into focus.

And also the Beat Museum founder & facilitator Jerry Cimino for all he's done for John and Carolyn over the decades, and for being the Beat Generation's longtime home base touchstone hearth.

On the New York end, I'd like to thank Walter Raubicheck and Levi Asher (now Marc Stein) for enthusiastically helping manifest so many shows in Manhattan for so many years, and Levi/Marc for his wild Madison Square Garden memory-story.

On the publishing end, I'd like to thank the bright light we're all lucky to be illuminated by, Holly George-Warren, for spearheading *The Rolling Stone Book of The Beats;* and Simon Warner & Jim Sampas for keeping the musical Beat alive with *Kerouac On Record.* And also out of England, Kevin Ring, for keeping the great *Beat Scene* magazine resonant & vibrant all these decades.

On the live show front — because that's a huge part of everything — I wanna thank Steve Edington, Cliff Whalen, Dan Bacon, Judith Bessette & all the other volunteers who for 30 years have made Lowell Celebrates Kerouac "the Woodstock of Jack" as I like to call it; and to the Wizard of Wonder (aka Chris Foster) and all his volunteer cohorts for keeping alive the Merry Pranksters Twanger Plunkers Family Reunion.

And also on the live show front — Still Will Bill Hodgson for the live Acid Tests he involved me in back in Winnipeg in the '70s, and for showing up at the Chelsea Commons in 2001 for Jack's 50th anniversary of writing *On The Road.*

On the photography end, I'd love to thank my Beat & Prankster pal and consummate photographic pro Jeremy Hogan, as well as my Swedish brother Johan Soderlund for digging through the old Amsterdam digital archives, plus all the other unknown friends and kind total strangers who took my camera and snapped an image so valuable it made it into a book!

I'd also like to thank David Wills — my Scottish brother in China helping this Canadian write about America — for all his book production skills and keen creative eye on all these different book projects we've shared.

Photo Credits

Front Cover —
John & Brian at the Rock n Roll Hall of Fame – unknown
fellow balcony denizen

John Section —
On The Road birthplace – 424 West 20th (p. 3) – by author
OTR 50th New York Show poster (p. 5) – by author
Kesey email (p. 6) – by author
Brian & Angela outdoors at night (p. 14) – unknown
Brian & Amram outdoors at night (p. 28) – unknown
Brian & Carolyn at desk on stage in Amsterdam (p. 32) –
unknown
Show poster (p. 34) – by S.A. Griffin
John in Venice Beach (p. 50) – by author
John at Hollywood sign (p. 71) – by author
Brian at scroll case in Christie's (p. 75) – unknown
Brian at scroll posters out front (p. 83) – unknown
Brian after the auction with Jim Irsay behind being
interviewed by the *New York Times* (p. 94) – unknown
Invitation to scroll debut party in Indiana (p. 96) – by author
Bixby Creek Bridge & beach (p. 99) – by author
John & Carolyn on stage in Amsterdam (p. 105) – unknown
Ferlinghetti's Big Sur cabin (p. 106) – by author
Brian, Walter, John & Jim in theater lobby (p. 114) – by
Jeremy Hogan
John on stage at The Bitter End (p. 116) – by John Grady

<u>Neal Section</u> —
Acid Test poster with all their names on it (p. 229) – by author
Allen's typed-up Six Gallery announcement (p. 237) – by author
The Rolling Stone Book of the Beats front cover (p. 250) – by author
The Electric Kool-Aid Acid Test front cover (p. 272) – by author
The Hitchhiker's Guide to Jack Kerouac covers (p. 292) – by author
How The Beats Begat The Pranksters covers (p. 293) – by author
Playing Woodstock (p. 295) – by author

<u>Back Cover</u> —
John & Brian with American flag (Sept. 2001) – unknown
The four of us holding hands in John's back yard in San Jose after his 50th birthday (Sept. 2001) – unknown

> I love the hand holds. They're not a limp
> "let's hold hands around a circle" hand
> grip — but a "I'm pulling you out of the
> rushing river hold on for dear life no
> fooling around" grip.

John & Carolyn on stage together (for the first time!) in Amsterdam (Nov. 1999) – unknown
Neal & Carolyn's ashes given to author by the family – by author

Index

The first two books of this Beat Trilogy
by Brian Hassett
The Hitchhiker's Guide to Jack Kerouac

"You did a fine job of bringing this back, far finer than my own memory, and I thought I had a decent one."

Dennis McNally
Kerouac & Grateful Dead scholar & author

"Both Kerouac and Hassett worked incredibly hard to seek out truth and beauty in this world. And then sat down and told us what they found. Read *The Hitchhiker's Guide* for the history. But don't miss the larger lessons within."

Kurt Landefeld
author of *Jack's Memoirs: Off The Road*

"A youthful memoir with all the never-to-be-recaptured frantic zest of a young man. Everything is wonderful in the Hassett world, even bad luck. Every cloud has a silver lining, and this attitude takes him far. It's the sheer unbridled enthusiasm that pours from Hassett that is so engaging."

Kevin Ring
Beat Scene Magazine

See 3 more pages of comments in front of book.

How The Beats Begat the Pranksters
& Other Adventure Tales

"Brian Hassett has made it his life's work to present to all of us the insights of the Beats and the Pranksters, and all the history, all the important things that came out of that, which have been perpetuated by the incredible vision, the incredible energy, of this man who is now one of our prime spokesmen, and we are so fortunate for that."

George Walker
original Merry Prankster and practicing Neal Cassady

"Brian Hassett doesn't just write ABOUT the Pranksters! He IS one! This book is great insider stuff about Ken Kesey and the Pranksters, about Jack Kerouac and the Beats, and especially about the late, great Neal Cassady, who did more than 'bridge the gap' between those two points in the Bohemian universe — he closed it!"

Lee Quarnstrom
author, journalist & original Merry Prankster

"This is an excellent new addition to the collective cultural canon from the People's Prankster Brian Hassett, Beat evangelist and voice of the living Dead. Our rocking roisterer and bebop brother has done it again."

Simon Warner
(author of *Text & Drugs & Rock n Roll* and *Kerouac on Record*)

Blissfully Ravaged in Democracy

"Loved this Hip Herodotus History of Happenings! You really nailed the whole era, in addition to a crash course in Pranksterland and your account of the afternoon tribute to Abbie. You show a new generation your take on the relationship of the THEN and the NOW, and that's the whole idea!"

David Amram
jazz bandleader, classical composer & Kerouac collaborator

"This book brings an insider perspective to what politics looks like on the ground, the human interaction, and what's really happening — when so much of this stuff gets erased by history. What is the reality of people involved in politics and how has it changed over the years? That's one of the interesting things that you get down in this book. It's continuing the theme of what you do. You're the Gonzo journalist type who's attracted to very interesting, colorful personalities, and you join them on their travels, and are able to communicate it so the reader feels like they're with you on these Adventures. It's a really fantastic thing that you're doing with your literary voice."

Mike Flynn
WUML DJ, musicologist, Beat scholar & festival coordinator